To my Loves

Some of this
Bit misogonistic but it . BASED
on **GODS** WORD. Now that I look
at it, I find it MAY NOT bE So much
as a helping tool. But as an
AFFIRMATION OF WHAT a GODly and
NOBLE woman you are. Thank you
For all that you are and all that
You've BECOME.

Your Soul Mate

A Woman of Noble Character

☙❧

Becoming a Proverbs 31 Woman in Today's Busy World

by

Susan Sikes

A woman of noble character, who can find?
She is worth far more than rubies.
Proverbs 31:10

AuthorHouse™
1663 Liberty Drive, Suite 200
Bloomington, IN 47403
www.authorhouse.com
Phone: 1-800-839-8640

AuthorHouse™ UK Ltd.
500 Avebury Boulevard
Central Milton Keynes, MK9 2BE
www.authorhouse.co.uk
Phone: 08001974150

First published by AuthorHouse 11/8/2006

ISBN: 1-4259-5774-9 (sc)

Printed in the United States of America
Bloomington, Indiana

This book is printed on acid-free paper.

Bloomington, IN   Milton Keynes, UK

authorHOUSE®

This project is in memory of my grandmother, "Granny Grace" Chapman, who lived the Proverbs 31 life. She not only showed me how to run a household, but most importantly, she was a living picture of how to love people.

As I reflect on her life, she is still teaching me things such as make time for people, cherish your relationships, family is everything, always be grateful, and enjoy serving all the people you come in contact with.

A Woman of Noble Character

The Proverbs 31 woman has been looked at as the perfect woman! The truth is that on this side of Heaven, there are no perfect people. The woman in Proverbs 31 is there to be an example for us; someone to look up to as a role model.

This woman has outstanding talents and qualities about her. I believe we all have some of the same outstanding talents and qualities. We have to dig deep and work to find out which ones God has given us and then use them to the best of our ability. When we do this, we will bring glory not only to our families, but also to God Himself!

It took me many years to understand the things discussed in this book. God has been doing an amazing work in me, and He started with changing my desires. Years ago, my desires were about myself and my career in teaching. My deepest desires are now about God, my family, and my home. In fact, this project came about when God took my desire to stay home and put it with my gift for teaching. He never ceases to amaze me!

After a couple years of teaching, and staying home during the summer months, I began to see what I had been missing as a housewife. I could also see how important staying home was to my family. Everything just seemed to run much smoother. I knew I needed some sort of income, so I tried many things. None seemed to work for me.

Every year, the desire God had placed within me grew. During the summer of 2004, I ran across a book by P.B. Wilson called, God is in the Kitchen Too. It had devotionals and recipes (which I cannot resist), so I bought it. This book was life changing for me! Not only did it talk about the importance of your kitchen ministry, it made me realize how many young women there were who had not been trained to be a wife or mother.

With so many women in the work force, housekeeping duties have fallen away or have been hired out. So many women of the past few generations have not even known how to cook when they got married. (I was included in this group). I truly believe that God led me to buy P.B. Wilson's book. While I was reading it, God spoke to me very clearly and told me that many women needed to be taught these things again. The very things I learned the hard way, through trial and error, I could teach others.

As I said, none of us are perfect. Therefore, we cannot be a perfect wife or mother. We will make mistakes, and we cannot do everything! When we do fall short of what we want to be or what we want to accomplish, I know God does not want us to live under guilt or condemnation. We can learn and grow from our shortcomings. As we take them to the Lord, He will help us be who He wants us to be.

 I could never say that I have mastered all of these things, but I am allowing God to teach me and help me grow in His timing. It is my prayer and desire that through this book, I can help other women be the wife God has called them to be. Go with me now to see God's example for us in the Proverbs 31 woman.

Prayerfully in His service,

Susan Sikes

By wisdom a house is built, and through understanding it is established; through knowledge its rooms are filled with rare and beautiful treasures.
Proverbs 24:3-4

A Woman of Noble Character

A woman of noble character, who can find?
    She is worth far more than rubies.
Her husband has full confidence in her
    And lacks nothing of value.
She brings him good, not harm,
    All the days of her life.
She selects wool and flax
    And works with eager hands.
She is like the merchant ships,
    Bringing her food from afar.
She gets up while it is still dark;
    She provides food for her family
    And portions for her servant girls.
She considers a field and buys it;
    Out of her earnings she plants a vineyard.
She sets about her work vigorously;
    Her arms are strong for her tasks.
She sees that her trading is profitable,
    And her lamp does not go out at night.
In her hand she holds the distaff
    And grasps the spindle with her fingers.
She opens her arms to the poor
    And extends her hands to the needy.
When it snows, she has no fear for her household;
    For all of them are clothed in scarlet.

She makes coverings for her bed;
    She is clothed in fine linen and purple.
Her husband is respected at the city gate,
    Where he takes his seat among the elders of the land.
She makes linen garments and sells them,
    And supplies the merchants with sashes.
She is clothed with strength and dignity;
    She can laugh at the days to come.
She speaks with wisdom,
    And faithful instruction is on her tongue.
She watches over the affairs of her household
    And does not eat the bread of idleness.
Her children arise and call her blessed;
    Her husband also, and he praises her:
"Many women do noble things,
    But you surpass them all."
Charm is deceptive, and beauty is fleeting;
    But a woman who fears the Lord is to be praised.
Give her the reward she has earned,
    And let her works bring her praise at the city gate.

Proverbs 31:10-31

Contents

Daily Priorities

When it snows, she has no fear for her household;
For all of them are clothed in scarlet.
Proverbs 31:21

She is clothed with strength and dignity;
She can laugh at the days to come.
She speaks with wisdom,
And faithful instruction is on her tongue.
She watches over the affairs of her household
And does not eat the bread of idleness.
Her children arise and call her blessed;
Her husband also, and he praises her:
"Many women do noble things,
But you surpass them all."
Charm is deceptive, and beauty is fleeting;
But a woman who fears the Lord is to be praised.
Give her the reward she has earned,
And let her works bring her praise at the city gate.

Proverbs 31:25-31

God

Always put **God** first in your life and in your marriage. Spend the first part of your day with Him in prayer and Bible reading. Ask for direction for your daily activities, strength for everything you have to do, and pray that you will be able to see each aspect of your life as worship.

Keep a prayer journal. This not only helps you remember who to pray for, but also lets you see God working in the lives of the people you pray for. You will see blessings all around you.

It is very important to be a part of a local church. The fellowship can be a very important aspect of your marriage. This is also where you will experience spiritual growth. The stronger you both are spiritually, the stronger your marriage will be.

Be a servant. Find out what your talents, abilities, passions, and gifts are and find a way to use them to glorify God. Not only will you bring glory to Him, but you will be more content with your life.

Love the Lord your God with all your heart and with all your soul and with all your strength.
Deuteronomy 6:5

So whether you eat or drink or whatever you do, do it all for the glory of God.
I Corinthians 10:31

Husbands

Set aside time each day to spend with your **husband**. Do not let your daily activities, career, or kids take the place of time with your husband.

Spend some time with your husband doing things that he enjoys. This does not have to be everyday, but show some interest in his hobbies.

Keep yourself attractive and appealing to your husband. Fix yourself up for him, even when it is just the 2 of you. Dress appropriately for him; public dress vs. private dress.

Observe your husband and find out what makes him feel loved the most. Once you find out, show affection in that manner. This may be pampering him, doting over him, loving on him physically (snuggling frequently), or doing extra things for him.

Submission is not a dirty word! Wives need to be submissive. This is not a slavery term. Submission is an attitude of being willing to put another's needs, desires, rights, and reputation ahead of our own to honor Christ. There is actually protection and order in being submissive. Husbands and wives should discuss and make decisions together. However, the husband should make the final decision in matters. Encourage him in these matters by being a supportive help-mate. This is what wives were designed to be.

Accept your husband's uniqueness; don't try to mold him. Don't be his mother or his conscience. Brag on him to others. Let him know you love, respect, admire, and appreciate him.

Wives, in the same way be submissive to your husbands so that, if any of them do not believe the word, they may be won over without words by the behavior of their wives, when they see the purity and reverence of your lives.
I Peter 3:1-2

In Conflict

Always remember that divorce is not an option. Too many people today go into a marriage with the attitude that if it doesn't work out, they will just get a divorce. Marriage is a sacred covenant!

Criticism, anger, defensiveness, walking away, arrogance, nagging, and unforgiveness are all characteristics that can kill a marriage. Stay away from these. Examine the situation and your part in it as well. Try to see the situation from your husband's point of view. Share your feelings while watching what you say and the manner in which you say it. A lot of conflicts can be handled easily with just a change in the tone of your voice. Talking softly and tenderly will keep the conversation at a moderate tone. It will also keep a calm spirit about both of you. Since marriage is an earthly picture of God's love, show mercy and grace instead of vengeance.

A gentle answer turns away wrath,
But harsh words stir up anger.
Proverbs 15:1

The Act of Marriage

Fatigue is a threat to a marriage. Weed out the unimportant things. You don't have to have and do it all. Don't let the stress of the day keep you from "loving" your husband. This is a vital part of your marriage!

Be desirable for your husband. Men are very visual creatures. Give him something nice to look at. There is a time for sweats and a T-shirt, but don't let that be all he sees you in each day. Fix your hair and your make-up for him as well. Good daily hygiene is also VERY important.

Keep things exciting for him. Don't get into the same ol' routine each time. Be the initiator on occasion.

Misconceptions:

Sex is just for men
It will never get better
Marriage can survive without it
It is a good reward

May your fountain be blessed,
And may you rejoice in the wife of your youth.
A loving doe, a graceful deer-
May her breasts satisfy you always,
May you ever be captivated by her love.
Proverbs 5:18-19

Children

Make your **children** and their activities a priority. Children need to feel that you sincerely care about them and what they do. Attend and be involved in their activities. Talk to your kids everyday, and be sure to LISTEN. Celebrate victories every chance you get. The earlier you get the lines of communication going, and consistently keep them open, the more your children will share as they grow. Treat them with respect, but remember that you are the parent. As they grow older, the relationship can turn more to a friendship. While they are young, they need to know you have authority.

Read to your kids everyday. This is vital in making them successful readers. Start while they are in the womb and never stop. As they get older, they can read to you as well.

Never criticize parents, grandparents, or teachers in front of the child.

Teach spiritual truths. Have your children drenched in the Word. Raise them in church and in a godly environment at home. The home words and actions need to match the words and actions at church.

Pray for them every day!

They need to feel important and loved in your eyes. Try to say at least 2 positive things each day to your children.

Don't always rescue them from their consequences.

Since children are a gift from God, we need to realize we are stewards and responsible for the way our children are raised.

Sons are a heritage from the Lord,
Children a reward from Him.
Psalm 127:3

Home

Your **home** needs to be a daily priority. Remember that our homes need to be an earthly picture of our Heavenly Home. It is very important that your home be clean, organized, comfortable, and peaceful. In keeping our homes in this manner, it will be a restful place for our families.

This will take work on a daily basis. Always remember that the yard is also part of your home. It should be kept neat and clean as well. Your yard is the first thing people see. Make a good first impression.

Make sure you have provisions for your family. Always be prepared for unexpected company or occasions. Keep the daily necessities in your home and feed your family good healthy meals. This too is an act of worship and servanthood.

Determine your best working time. If you are a morning person, you will probably be more productive in the morning. Schedule your tasks around your body's timetable. Make out a daily schedule to use as a guide. Use the schedule to help you get all daily things accomplished.

If you are able to work at home, you may need to make up a weekly or all day schedule. After a period of time, it will become a habit. Find the one that works best for you.

Ex.	5:00 A.M.	Wake up/Get coffee
	5:10 A.M.	Go over the schedule for the day
	5:15 A.M.	Prayer time and Bible Reading
	6:15 A.M.	Wake up husband with coffee/Watch the news
	6:30 A.M.	Shower and get ready for the day
	7:00 A.M.	Leave for work

Keep a peaceful attitude in your home. Watch the tone in which you respond to people. Notice if your tone is different with your boss than with your family. If is it, something is wrong. Even in times when someone else is angry, you can control the situation with a gentle answer. Remember Proverbs 15:1 which was quoted earlier.

People are more likely to honor your requests if you ask in a nice way. They are also more likely to do things for you if you are constantly putting them first. This makes a big difference in a relationship. Always set the example that Christ set for us. He had a sacrificing love and put the world before His own comfort and desires.

The wise woman builds her house,
But with her own hands the foolish one tears hers down.
Proverbs 14:1

By wisdom a house is built,
And through understanding it is established;
Through knowledge its rooms are filled
With rare and beautiful treasures.
Proverbs 24:3,4

Yourself

Be sure to set time aside for **yourself**. You may not have a lot of extra time in this area, but 5 minutes here and there will help you stay balanced. If there are hobbies or activities that you enjoy, try to make time for these, within reason. Even reading a book in a bubble bath at the end of the day can do wonders for you. Make sure you don't spend so much time doing your own thing that you end up neglecting your family.

If you work from home, try to get out at least once a week. You could join a Bible study at church, do some volunteer work, or just go shopping or have lunch with a friend. There are Mother's Day Out programs that can help with the kids. There is no need to feel guilty about this. The kids will love it.

Examine your character! Being able to keep a clean, organized house and having the ability to serve up delicious meals will mean nothing if your character is not what it should be. If what you do for your family is not done with a willing and sweet spirit, there will be an aura of bitterness about it. Your family will not be able to rest and enjoy all that you have done to the fullest.

Better a meal of vegetables where there is love
Than a fattened calf with hatred.
Proverbs 15:17

A wife of noble character is her husband's crown,
But a disgraceful wife is like decay in his bones.
Proverbs 12:4

The Character of a Godly Woman

Teach the older women to be reverent in the way they live, not to be slanderers or addicted to much wine, but to teach what is good. Then they can train the younger women to love their husbands and children, to be self-controlled and pure, to be busy at home, to be kind, and to be subject to their husbands, so that no one will malign the Word of God. Titus 2:4-5

Have an "Others First" Attitude

We are called to be Christ-like. To do this, we have to know the character of Christ. When you look back into the scriptures, everything He did was about serving others. He spoke kindly, worked miracles among people, continued to minister to people even when he was exhausted, returned insults with kind words, washed the disciples feet, and ultimately gave His own life for our sakes.

When we put everything into perspective, some of the things we get upset about seem rather trivial. When you see yourself beginning to get upset over a situation, think about the reason. If the words "I" "Me", and "My" keep coming up, ask yourself truly what Jesus would do in the situation.

Do nothing out of selfish ambition or vain conceit, but in humility consider others better than yourselves. Each of you should look not only to your own interests, but also to the interests of others.
Philippians 2:3-4

Be devoted to one another in brotherly love. Honor one another above yourselves.
Romans 12:10

Be Kind

Another characteristic of Christ that we need to follow is His kindness. Our words and actions should be seasoned with kindness. If we are speaking or acting in a way that does not exhibit kindness, we look just like the world.

Unkind words and actions can deeply hurt people. The real tragedy is that although we may work in this area when we are in the workplace, church, or other public areas, we tend to let our guard down at home. When this happens, it is our family we are hurting!

Kindness is contagious. My family has actually conducted an experiment in this area. Our two children were constantly in some type of conflict. We approached my daughter and talked to her about some kind things she could do for her brother. This included words and actions. The first day, my son was a little skeptical, but after that he began doing nice things for her. He even bought her gifts. It was as if they were actually friends who were trying to see who could outdo the other in the area of kindness.

I have had to work with people who were very hard to get along with. After consistently showing kindness, they softened up and were easier to work with. The key was "consistently" showing kindness, even when they were unkind. Sometimes this is extremely difficult. The only way to master it is to ask God for help.

A kind man benefits himself,
But a cruel man brings trouble on himself.
Proverbs 11:17

Be Trustworthy & Truthful

Being honest is an area of utmost importance. If the Lord is Truth and Satan is the father of lies, we need to examine ourselves and see exactly whom it is that we are following.

Once you have a reputation for lying, people will not trust you. This is a hard cycle to break. It may take a long time of proving your honesty to them before they will actually believe you. Without trust in a relationship, you have practically nothing!

Some areas of dishonesty:

Falsehoods/Lies
Gossip
Exaggerated stories
False flattery
Omission of the truth

The Lord detests lying lips,
But He delights in men who are truthful.
Proverbs 12:22

Be Energetic

If we are going to be the women God has called us to be, we have to be energetic. Being able to take care of our families' needs requires lots of energy. We have to be ready to attack whatever responsibility comes our way.

If we have a sluggish attitude toward our responsibilities, we will not be able to accomplish all we need to do. We will also send a negative message to our families. Try to be excited about serving them.

This does not mean you cannot delegate some of the responsibilities to other family members. However, remember that attitudes are contagious. If we start out with a negative or sluggish attitude, our families could very easily have the same attitude. On the other hand, if we have a positive outlook and attack the tasks with enthusiasm, our families may also follow the positive attitude.

The sluggard craves and gets nothing,
But the desires of the diligent are fully satisfied.
Proverbs 13:4

He who works his land will have abundant food,
But he who chases fantasies will have his fill of poverty.
Proverbs 28:19

Be Patient

Patience goes hand in hand with kindness. We have to practice patience. It seems that the times we need to practice patience the most are the times we have the least amount of it. When our lack of patience turns to anger, and our anger goes into action, we sin.

When we lose our patience with people, anger comes out. Sometimes this anger is a result of other circumstances that have been building up, and not due to the person that we end up taking it out on. However, the person who receives the brunt of our anger or frustration will feel as though they have caused the stressful situation.

Occasionally, we will need patience in dealing with a particular person. If there is a person who is hard for you to deal with, communicate with them. This can be the key to resolving the entire issue. Be honest with them, but speak in a loving manner.

Again, it is very easy to control our temper with people outside of our families. We should do the same within our families. Flying off the handle should never be acceptable. An apology will help, but the hurt will still be there.

An angry man stirs up dissension,
And a hot-tempered one commits many sins.
Proverbs 29:22

A man's wisdom gives him patience;
It is to his glory to overlook an offense.
Proverbs 19:11

Be Prudent

Growing up, I always heard the virtue of prudence in a negative manner. I can remember the picture of a stiff-necked person having no fun. They were called prudes.

Actually, prudence is a good quality to have. I looked in the Thesaurus to get some synonyms for the word. I found that it meant discretion, carefulness, caution, tact, and foresight. All of these are qualities we should strive for. These basic parts of wisdom have nothing to do with not having fun. It is all about making wise choices for you and your family. It is about protecting your family as you pray about and think through decisions.

Prudence is about seeking God's will for your life and the life of your family. In seeking God's will for our families, we will experience great joy.

I, wisdom, dwell together with prudence;
I possess knowledge and discretion.
Proverbs 8:12

The prudent see danger and take refuge,
But the simple keep going and suffer for it.
Proverbs 27:12

Be Self-Controlled

We are all called to live self-controlled or disciplined lives. This affects every aspect of our being. We have to use self-control for everything from cleaning the house to dealing with the people around us.

Each person has strengths and weaknesses in different areas. The first step in being disciplined is recognizing where you need the help. Once you know which areas you are struggling with, lift them to God. Ask Him for help in conquering those aspects of your life. Let your self-control be God-control.

With man this is impossible,
But with God all things are possible.
Matthew 19:26

Areas in which we may need more self-control or discipline than others:

Getting out of bed in the morning
Turning off the TV
Shopping or NOT shopping
Living beyond our means
Keeping up with duties
Watching our mouths
Complaining or being negative
Exercise
Eating habits
Daily quiet time with God
Putting others first

The woman Folly is loud;
She is undisciplined and without knowledge.
Proverbs 9:13

Like a city whose walls are broken down
Is a man who lacks self-control.
Proverbs 25:28

Fear God

Throughout the Bible, it tells us to "Fear God." This is talking about a reverential fear. We are not to be afraid of Him, but to worship Him in awe and reverence. We should lift Him up above all other people and things, letting nothing come before Him.

When we truly see who He is and what He has done for each one of us, we will have a reverential fear for Him. At this point, we will want to live in obedience to Him. When we "Fear God," we strive to obey Him!

The fear of the Lord is the beginning of wisdom,
And knowledge of the Holy One is understanding.
Proverbs 9:10

Humility and the fear of the Lord
Bring wealth and honor and life.
Proverbs 22:4

Watch How You Talk

Your true character comes out in what you say. Words are powerful and can have a negative or positive affect on you and the people around you. Words can tear people down, or build them up. As women striving to please God, we should purpose to build not only our families up, but the people around us also. This is one of the most difficult areas for people to master. The Bible talks about being able to control large animals and ships, but not being able to control our tongues.

Always keep a tight rein on your tongue. The Bible has many verses addressing this aspect of our character. Watching what we say includes the tone that we use when speaking to others, spreading things that we hear, griping or complaining, and the actual content of what we say. All of these areas should reflect the character of Christ.

Another area concerning words that we need to be aware of is our self-conversations. We normally do not consider the things we think to ourselves as conversations; however that is exactly what they are. You can talk yourself into being offended or mad at someone just by dwelling on an incident or thinking negative things about that person. Just because your words are not audible doesn't mean they won't have an ill effect on people.

Several years ago, someone gave me a checklist to examine my words. Ask yourself these questions BEFORE you say anything or as you find yourself thinking:

1. **Is it kind?**
2. **Is it true?**
3. **Is it necessary?**
4. **Does it reflect Christ's Character?**

If the answer to any of these questions is "No", refrain from saying them and purpose to redirect your thoughts.

He who guards his mouth and tongue
Keeps himself from calamity.
Proverbs 21:23

Watch How You Dress

Modesty should always be an issue for women. Fashions today are too revealing, but accepted by people of all ages. Women should dress in a way that reflects God in their lives! God's Word tells us not to conform to the world, but to be transformed. If a certain fashion looks like the world, let the world wear it. You can dress in a Godly manner and still be attractively dressed.

I also want women to dress modestly, with decency and propriety...
I Timothy 2:9

The Bible also says not to cause a person to stumble in sin. Some of the revealing fashions of today are so revealing that men may find themselves lusting. I have heard women say that if a man has a problem with lust, that is his own problem. However, the Bible says something different. We are responsible and sin if we cause someone else to stumble.

Be careful, however, that the exercise of your freedom does not become a stumbling block to the weak.
I Corinthians 8:9

When you sin against you brothers in this way and wound their weak conscience, you sin against Christ.
I Corinthians 8:12

Don't let this keep you from dressing in a desirable way for your husband, in the privacy of your own home.

Decorating Your Home

In her hand she holds the distaff
And grasps the spindle with her fingers.
Proverbs 31:19

She makes coverings for her bed;
She is clothed in fine linen and purple.
Proverbs 31:22

Have you heard the expression, "Bloom where you are planted?" Keep this expression in mind when you think about your living conditions. There will be times (especially in the beginning of your marriage) that you are not in your "dream home." Be faithful with what you have.

Years ago I lived through a period where most of my friends were in new or larger homes than I was. I was not bitter or envious, but I did desire to have a nicer house. I kept my house picked up and cleaned, but didn't really do any decorating or extras. God gave me a verse to live by:

'Well done, my good servant!' his master replied. 'Because you have been trustworthy in a very small matter, take charge of ten cities.'

This really started to make sense to me when a good friend of mine sold her house and moved into a rent house while they built another one. While she was in the rental property, she painted and put up new wallpaper. She kept it clean, organized, and decorated. Seeing the way she responded to a temporary situation made a lasting impression on me. Bloom where you are planted!

Enjoy, appreciate, decorate, and take care of what God gives you at the time. Be patient and faithful with what you have and in His timing, more will come.

Decorating Tips

- The most important aspect of decorating your house is to always remember that it should reflect your family's personality and the things you enjoy. You may not have much experience in decorating. You may not even realize what you like when you begin decorating. Finding out your style is the first step. To do this, watch as many decorating shows on TV as possible (HGTV is filled with great shows), look through home magazines, tour model homes, and look at friends and neighbors' homes. It will be easy to see what style you are drawn to.

- Decide on the colors you like. This will help as you are planning and shopping. Again, the colors you choose need to reflect who you are and what you like. All rooms do not have to have the same color scheme. However, a good rule to use is that if you can see one room from another, try to have at least one common color to tie the rooms together.

- When choosing colors, keep in mind that lighter-toned colors make the room appear larger, while darker colors make them seem smaller.

- Mirrors also make rooms appear larger than they are.

- The basic rule for hanging pictures is to hang it at the average eye level. Be careful if you very short or tall. Your eye level may not be what most people will see as eye level.

- Decorating your home on a budget is much easier than it sounds. Before you buy anything, shop, shop, shop. Many times you can find the same items at discount stores for much less. Garage sales and thrift stores can be beneficial as well. If you buy something used, be sure it is in good condition. You can always refinish an object or paint it, but it must be sturdy.

- Ebay is another good source. Beware of shipping charges and read all of the description.

- Many items can be made. Be creative. When you see things, look at all the possibilities. Tables do not have to be used as tables, almost anything can be made into a lamp or clock, and there is an unlimited amount of items to hang on the wall. Just be sure before you buy something, you really like it.

- Once you have an area decorated, step back and look again. Be sure everything looks right. If not, move it around until you like it. Also, walk in your front door to see your house as visitors see it. This can be eye opening. Remember, this is their first impression of your home.

- Be sure to keep walkways open. It should be easy to get from room to room.

- Fresh flowers always brighten up a room. To make your own arrangements, criss-cross tape across the top of a wide mouthed vase and insert the stems in the openings. Be sure to remove any leaves that will be below the water line. Keep flowers away from direct sunlight or air vents.

- Use things in your decorating that mean something to you. Heirlooms and special gifts do not need to be tucked away, display them. However, if you have small children, keep breakables out of reach.

- Lamps change the whole appearance of a room. The lighting from a lamp gives the room a more welcoming and cozy atmosphere.

- Candles are another inexpensive way to decorate. Candle light gives off a romantic flare. With scented candles, the house will not only look great, but will smell great also.

- If you have any type of item made of white fabric and would prefer it to be off-white or cream colored, soak it in coffee or tea for about 15 minutes. For large items, pour pots of coffee into the kitchen sink to soak them. Wash them in the washing machine, without detergent 1st. If you do not like the look, wash it again with bleach in the water, and most fabrics will return to white.

Keeping Your House Clean

Making our homes an earthly picture of our Heavenly Home

She sets about her work vigorously;
Her arms are strong for her tasks.
Proverbs 31:17

She watches over the affairs of her household
And does not eat the bread of idleness.
Proverbs 31:27

Making our homes an earthly picture of our Heavenly Home

P.B. Wilson calls your home God's embassy. She relates it to ambassadors living in foreign countries. Although they are away from their homeland, their embassy has sites, smells, and objects from home. Our homes should reflect our real embassy, Heaven.

This gives a whole new attitude towards keeping our homes clean and organized. We should do it as if we were doing it for God. As you think about representing God in our homes, it really gives you the desire to do your best at keeping it clean.

We are stewards for the things that God blesses us with. Our homes are definitely blessings! We should take the best care possible, regardless of the size, condition, type of dwelling, or location of our homes.

Housework

These household chores are just listed as a guideline. Each home is different. For some people they will feel the need to do some of these more often, while other people will do each chore less than what is listed. Find out what you feel is appropriate for your house.

There is a checklist entitled, <u>Household Cleaning Jobs</u> in the Appendix that we use on cleaning days. This lists everything that needs to be done. Most of the time, the kids assign themselves certain jobs. However, everyone in the house can do a check to see what jobs are remaining.

- Get into a cleaning system. You have to find out what works best for you. As I was growing up, my mother worked outside our home. As a result, we set aside most Saturday mornings to do all the house cleaning. This is still effective. However, since I teach school and I am off in the summer, my schedule is somewhat different. We do the cleaning during the week. I have done this 2 different ways, and have not decided what works best for me at this point.

1st – Set aside 1 day during the week to do all major house cleaning. The other days are for maintaining and running errands.

2nd – Make a list of cleaning jobs to be done during the week. Divide them out among the 5 weekdays. Do a few jobs each day so that none of your days are overwhelmed with housework.

For deep Spring Cleaning (once a year), you can either set aside a day as mentioned for daily cleaning, or break it down also. Take 1 room or closet a day and do a thorough deep cleaning.

Daily Jobs:

Make beds
Straighten rooms
Dishes
Laundry as needed
Kitchen Countertops

Monthly Jobs:

Clean top of refrigerator
Clean mirrors
Clean off porches & patios
Wipe down all windowsills
Change air filters
Check fire alarm batteries

Weekly Jobs:

Water plants
Dust all furniture
Laundry
Sweep
Mop
Vacuum
Change sheets on all beds
Bathrooms
Yard Work

Deep Cleaning Jobs:
(once or twice a year)

Clean all baseboards
Clean ceiling fans and light fixtures
Dust any hard to reach shelves
Clean behind appliances
Clean cobwebs out of corners
Clean blinds
Clean windows
Wash throws, table cloths, lace, curtains, or linens that are kept out

Cleaning Tips

- Try to put things in their place as you finish with them. This keeps you rom having such an overwhelming task later. 'If the entire family is trained to pick up their own things, you will have more time for other things.

- In going along with picking things up and putting them in the proper place, make sure this is done each night before going to bed. It sets a better tone in the morning when you wake up to an orderly house.

- Try to set aside time in the morning to make beds and clear away any breakfast dishes before leaving the house. Again, this sets a nicer tone when you walk in the door.

- Clean from top to bottom. In other words, if you are cleaning ceiling fans, clean them before you dust or vacuum. You should dust and wipe off countertops before vacuuming.

- Start off doing the things you like best. This can actually get you in more of a "cleaning mood." As for the chores you dislike, set a goal each day to finish 1 of these chores.

- Bleach works great to remove mold and mildew from showers.

- Emilie Barnes has a great system for using your time wisely. She says to keep a list of 5 minute or less chores. While commercials are on, or when you only have a couple of minutes, you can do some of the items on your list. (taking out the trash, cleaning mirrors, watering the plants, feeding the animals, or cleaning a toilet)

- Get the family involved. As kids get older, they need to have age appropriate chores. This not only teaches responsibility, but it gives them a sense of worth in the family. Try not to redo their chore, at least in front of them. As they get older, you can expect better quality work. If they are capable and do not do it correctly, make them redo it.

- To clean shower doors, use distilled white vinegar.

- Be sure to have a sink of dishwater ready while you are cooking as well as while you are eating. While you cook, either soak the dishes as you go, or go ahead and put them in the dishwasher. After the meal, your job will be more manageable. As each family member leaves the table, they can scrape the leftovers off of their plate and put it in the sink full of dishwater. This is no trouble for each person, but will save you a lot of time and steps going back and forth to clear off the table. If you are not able to get to the dishes immediately, the water will keep the food from drying onto the dishes.

- If you find out that you are having unexpected company and do not have time to do heavy cleaning, here are a few tips:

  A. Get a laundry basket and collect clutter that needs to be put away. Put the basket in a hidden room until you can unload it later.
  B. Make sure the bathrooms are cleaned.
  C. If there is no time for the bathrooms, do a quick wipe down and put ½ a cup of bleach in the toilets.
  D. Light some candles.

- Go through your things periodically and get rid of unwanted or out grown items. If they are things you want to save, store them in a labeled box, in the attic.

- Read directions on all cleaning chemicals. Follow them closely. If they are used incorrectly, some of them can be very dangerous to your health.

- To clean silk arrangements or hard to dust items, spray them with Lysol. It eats the dust right off. For some fabrics or materials, you might try it on a small piece to make sure it doesn't damage or discolor it. If this doesn't work, blow the dust off regularly with a hairdryer.

- Jewelry can be soaked in sudsy ammonia overnight. The next morning brush it off gently with an old toothbrush and rinse thoroughly. This works just as well as high priced jewelry cleaner.

- Leave an extra trash bag or two in the bottom of the trashcan. When you take the trash out, you already have the next liner available.

- Keep a box or basket by the garage door for wet or muddy shoes. Line the bottom of it with a trash bag.

- Clean your coffee maker thoroughly at least once a month. To do this, pour equal amounts of water and distilled vinegar through the cycle. Run another cycle of just water to rinse it out.

- To eliminate odors in the kitchen sink, run citrus peels through the garbage disposal.

- To keep a sink from clogging, pour ½ a cup of baking soda into the drain and follow with hot water.

- Always try to dry off the shower doors and bathroom fixtures after each use. This will keep them looking clean longer.

- If you have a hairspray film on your bathroom mirror, try cleaning it with rubbing alcohol.

- Change your air filters regularly. Each house is different. Check them monthly to see if they need to be changed. This will save energy as well as keep the dust in the house down.

- Try to clean windows on cloudy days instead of sunny ones. The sun will cause the windows to streak.

- When washing windows, clean with horizontal strokes on the inside and vertical strokes on the outside. This way, when there is a streak, you will be able to tell which side it is on.

- Place all large pots or pans in the top rack of the dishwasher. If you put them on the bottom, they will block the water from reaching the items on the top.

Laundry Tips

- When doing laundry, always run the water and let it get sudsy before putting the clothes in.

- Check all care labels in clothing before washing. Make sure the items are not hand wash or dry clean only.

- When using bleach, pour it into the water before adding the laundry. Never pour bleach directly onto clothing.

- Wash like colors together: Dark clothes, Light colored clothes, and Towels & Linens.

- Be sure to check all pockets before putting articles in the washing machine. Gum, pens, and other things can ruin an entire load of laundry.

- Take clothes out of the dryer immediately. This will help keep them from wrinkling. If you do not catch it in time, put a wet towel in the dryer with the clothes and restart for a few minutes.

- Clean out the lint filter of the dryer after each use. This will save drying time.

- Do not over load the dryer or the clothes will be wrinkled regardless of when you remove them. Also, shake each article of clothing out before putting them into the dryer. This will also reduce wrinkles.

- If at all possible, try to set up some type of clothesline to hang the clothes on when you get them out of the dryer. Keep hangers available. Hang each family members' clothing together when you take them out. When you are ready to take them to individual rooms, you don't have to sort them. This will save time and cut down on the wrinkles.

- When hanging up tank tops or sleeveless items, use wire coat hangers. Bend the top part of the hanger to make a valley on each side so the clothing will not slip off the end of the hanger.

Finances

She considers a field and buys it;
Out of her earnings she plants a vineyard.
Proverbs 31:16

She opens her arms to the poor
And extends her hands to the needy.
Proverbs 31:20

She makes linen garments and sells them,
And supplies the merchants with sashes.
Proverbs 31:24

First and foremost, you must give God His portion (10%) first. This is Biblical and vital to managing your money.

> *"Bring the whole tithe into the storehouse, that there may be food in My house. Test Me in this," says the Lord Almighty, "and see if I will not throw open the floodgates of Heaven and pour out so much blessing that you will not have room enough for it. I will prevent pests from devouring your crops, and the vines in your fields will not cast their fruit," says the Lord Almighty. "Then all the nations will call you blessed, for yours will be a delightful land," says the Lord Almighty. Malachi 3:10-12*

> *Remember this: Whoever sows sparingly will also reap sparingly, and whoever sows generously will also reap generously. Each man should give what he has decided in his heart to give, not reluctantly or under compulsion, for God loves a cheerful giver. And God is able to make all grace abound to you, so that in all things at all times, having all that you need, you will abound in every good work. 2 Corinthians 9:6-8*

** GOD WILL BLESS YOUR OBEDIENCE! Tithing is a matter of obedience, as well as a matter of trust.

Wise Spending

- Don't live beyond your means. Know your income and expenses and do not let your expenses outweigh your income. Come up with a budget that fits your family's needs. Allow a certain amount for eating out, hobbies, going out, ... Spreadsheets work wonderfully.

- Going along with living within your means is realizing that more than likely, you will not start off in the same financial lifestyle as when you left your parents. Keep in mind that it probably took your parents at least your lifetime to get to where they are financially. Many people get married and try to buy the same things, and in the same amounts as when it was their parents' money. This can create a huge debt that will take years to pay off.

Credit

- Do NOT charge items on credit cards unless you pay them off monthly. This is a trap most people fall into. The interest will destroy your bank account. You will end up paying more for the item than it is worth.
Joyce Meyer gives a very wise saying to teach this subject. She says,

- "If you use credit cards without paying them off monthly, you are using tomorrow's prosperity today. When tomorrow comes, there won't be any prosperity left."

- If you do use a credit card or cards and pay them off monthly, be sure you are using one with a return built into it. There are many that pay you up to 5% on all purchases.

- Also, keep a record on your computer or at home with your credit card information on it. Be sure to include the company's name, address, phone #, date of expiration, and interest rate. The interest rate is for your information, but the other would be needed if the card was lost or stolen.

- If you have to finance things (cars, houses, appliances...) shop around for not only the best prices, but the best interest rates, and lowest fees. These can save you thousands of dollars over the years.

- Be sure to pay all bills on time. Your credit means so much. With a bad credit rating, you are not always able to purchase things such as cars and houses that need to be financed. If you do get financing, the interest is very high. However, with good credit, you not only can finance things, but you can actually get a lower interest rate.

- To make sure bills are paid on time, mail them several days before they are due. Set aside specific days to pay your bills. This can be done once a week or twice a month, whatever works best with your pay schedule.

- After you have finished paying off a loan, continue paying the same amount either to your savings account, or put the extra amount on the principle balance of another loan.

Savings and Investments

- If at all possible, set aside money for a savings account. If you can set aside 10% of your income to go into a savings account, you will not have to finance items as much. This is also great for a Christmas fund. Too many people go into debt buying Christmas presents for their families. Most people do not want you to get in debt to get them a gift! Celebrate the true meaning of Christmas. This does not mean you shouldn't buy your loved ones gifts, but be reasonable. For others, such as co-workers and casual friends, homemade gifts and baked items are so appreciated.

- If you are fortunate enough to have an employer who provides you with Retirement options, take full advantage of the situation. This is hard when you are young, because retirement seems so far away. Think long term so you will be able to live comfortably when you get older.

- Beware of scams!!!! There are so many "Get Rich Quick" schemes. The ones who are getting rich quick are the ones scamming people. Be skeptical of all situations and fully investigate before putting any money into a business opportunity. Read ALL fine print, pray about all ventures, don't let your emotions/greed make your decisions for you, and always remember that if someone tells you it is a now or never opportunity, pass it up!

Financial Tips

- Weigh your options when it comes to finances. Decide what you can afford and stick to that amount. If a maid is of the utmost importance to you, figure that into your budget, but give up something else. If DSL is important to you and you can afford it, go for it. If you can't afford it, give something else up that is not vital. You can save money by doing all of your own laundry and ironing instead of using a dry cleaners. Don't try to have it all!

- To make a little extra money when clothes are outgrown, take them to a consignment shop or have a garage sale. If you would rather, you can donate them to an organization. If you donate them, be sure to get a receipt. The amount will be tax deductible.

- Buy Christmas wrapping paper and decorations after Christmas for the next year. This will save you a bundle.

- Be sure to balance your bank statements as soon as you get them. This will point out any mistakes early on, which can save you money on fees if you have insufficient funds.

- To save money on landscaping, plant perennials. They will come back year after year. There are some annual flowers, such as zinnias, that you can save the seeds for the next year. To do this, cut off the dead flower heads and save them in a brown paper sack in a dark dry place until the next Spring. When the time comes, sprinkle them into your flowerbeds. You will have a garden full of flowers at no expense.

- When making a purchase that has a rebate, always fill out the information to get your money. Keep a copy of all forms, receipts, and proof of purchases. Record the date you mailed the information, and make note of the telephone number to call if you have questions. If the rebate doesn't come within the specified time, call and check on it.

- Always watch for extra fees when using ATMs. Try to find one with no charges. They really add up quickly.

- When starting home improvement projects, check into doing it yourself. Research it well before hiring someone else to do the job for you. However, don't get in over your head.

Do it Yourself to Save Money

Laundry instead of dry cleaners
Wash your car instead of going to a car wash
Change your own oil for ½ the price
Do your own minor car repairs
Cook your own meals instead of eating out
Rent a DVD instead of going to the movie
Clean your own house instead of maid service

Shopping

She selects wool and flax
And works with eager hands.
Proverbs 31:13

She is like the merchant ships,
Bringing her food from afar.
Proverbs 31:14

She considers a field and buys it;
Out of her earnings she plants a vineyard.
Proverbs 31:16

She sees that her trading is profitable,
And her lamp does not go out at night.
Proverbs 31:18

Shopping

Shopping for a family can be an overwhelming experience. It is important that you keep it as simple and inexpensive as possible. Here are a few ideas to help in this area.

Emilie Barnes suggests keeping a spreadsheet with all of the meals your family enjoys. When you are trying to decide on the menu for the week, let them have a part in choosing meals. (See the Appendix for an example of the spreadsheet that includes all meals.)

After you have all the meals chosen, make a menu for the week. You can post this chart on the refrigerator to serve as a reminder to you. Your family will also know when they are having their favorite meals. (See Appendix for the Weekly Menu Chart.)

Looking at your menu for the week, make a shopping list that includes all items you will need. Don't forget paper products, cleaning supplies, and personal hygiene items. You can do this several different ways. You can simply make a list of all items, or use a variety of charts.

I have a shopping chart with most of the things I buy on a regular basis. I actually have 2 different versions. The 1st is a generic list that is applicable to any store. The topics are listed by like items. The 2nd is a list that is applicable to my local Wal-Mart store only. I have each isle listed and the items I buy on a regular basis listed as they are in the store. The only issue with this list is that stores frequently rearrange items. However, keeping my list updated and using it regularly saves me lots of time and frustration. If I have each thing I need checked off, I never have to double back in the store. (Both lists can be found in the Appendix).

Shopping Tips

- Comparison Shopping – Always compare sizes/weight to prices of each brand. Some items you never want to skimp on. However, most are fine to buy the generic brand. You have to find out what is important and works for you.

- Using Coupons – Clip and save coupons for added savings. Watch for the expiration dates. Be careful though, some generic brands are less expensive than the name brands, even with a coupon.

- Shopping with competitive ads – Watch for weekly ads and mark the things you need. You can either make a list of what each store has, or circle the actual ads. Take your lists and ads to stores that honor other competitor's prices, such as Wal-Mart, and take advantage of all sale prices.

- Stocking up during clearances– Watch for clearance racks! These are not only great for clothes, but watch all store areas for future gifts. Think ahead for birthdays, Christmas, bridal and baby showers, etc…

- Keep a list of gift ideas– Keep a list of ideas for different family members who are hard to buy for. As things are mentioned in conversations, jot them down so you will have ideas when it is gift-giving time. I keep mine in my planner, but you could just keep it in your purse. You may want to list their hobbies, favorite colors, and sizes as well. You never know when a favorite item will be on the clearance rack.

- Buying in bulk– Be sure to check prices with quantity. Usually, bulk is much cheaper, not to mention that your supply will last much longer.

- Make 1 large shopping trip instead of going daily– If at all possible, try to purchase all items for the week or more in one trip. When you go daily, you end up buying more items and spending more money. Throughout the week, keep a list of things you need, as you realize you are almost out. This will assure that you get all things in 1 trip.

- Try to stay with the list, without buying a lot of extras. If at all possible, try not to go to the store when you are hungry. You will tend to buy more.

- Try to shop during the least busy times. This will keep your nerves from being shot! You will also be able to think more clearly to make the best purchases.

- Always buy foods with the longest expiration date.

- As I think of things I want or need for the house, my family, or myself, I write it down on a list that I keep in my planner. I always have it at hand while I am out shopping. This is similar to my gift ideas list.

- When greeting cards of any kind are on sale, buy them. Some non-profit organizations send them through the mail. Organize them by topics in a box. When an occasion comes up or takes you by surprise, you will be prepared.

- Look at thrift stores and garage sales. I have found top quality items and expensive antiques for pennies at garage sales and thrift stores. Be sure to check the condition of the items. If you are looking for books, Salvation Army sells all books and magazines for 25 cents! I purchase new books with the stickers still on them for 25 cents on a regular basis.

- When shopping for clothing, and trying to match something, take the item with you. Most stores will allow you to carry things in for matching purposes. Just be sure to let someone know as you go into the store. They may put a special sticker on it.

Homemade Gift
Baskets and Ideas

*Each man should give what he has decided in his heart
to give, not reluctantly or under compulsion,
For God loves a cheerful giver.
2 Corinthians 9:7*

Homemade Gift Baskets and Ideas

Pie Fixin's

In a pie plate, place a rolling pin, pie crust (rolled in waxed paper), dry ingredients in a jar, apples, and recipe to an apple pie. You can include any other items that would be helpful. Wrap the items in a pretty kitchen towel.

Cookie Dough...

When you make cookie dough, make extra. Roll it into a nice sized roll and cover it with parchment paper. Tie the ends up with ribbon. Keep it in the freezer until ready to use or give. For a gift, provide a roll or 2 of frozen cookie dough with a baking sheet, spatula, and or cookie cutters. The dough will keep for about 2 months in the freezer.

Canned Items

Any type of canned foods make great gifts. When giving canned foods, decorate the jar by putting a pretty fabric between the lid and the seal. Add some ribbon and a tag or label to tell what the item is.

Bucket of Spaghetti

Take a bucket and line it with a dishtowel. Add all the things needed to make fresh spaghetti and sauce. You will need spaghetti, tomatoes, basil, garlic, French bread, Parmesan cheese, and possibly a flower for the table.

Scented Sugars

In a canning or decorative jar, layer granulated sugar with scented, edible items. You can use rose petals, vanilla beans, scented-geranium leaves, or citrus peel. If you use citrus peel, set it out to dry for a day before adding it to the sugar. Seal the jars tightly and let them set for a few days. The scents will infuse the sugar. Place a nice label on the jar for a special touch.

Baked Items

Any baked foods (breads, cakes, cookies…) are always appreciated.

Hot Chocolate or Coffee Basket

Fill a basket with mugs, hot chocolate, coffee, marshmallows, sugar, cinnamon, creamer, cookies and/or a small cake.

Cornbread Gift

One of the most thoughtful gifts my mother ever gave me had to do with making cornbread. She gave us a cast iron skillet and the recipe to her homemade cornbread mix. With this, she included several premixed bags of the dry ingredients. All we had to do was add the liquid and bake.

Cook's Gift Basket

Fill a large basket with items used for cooking. Include kitchen gadgets, cookbooks, kitchen towels, spices, and even ingredients for a specific recipe. You can have specific themes for each basket. For example, a barbecue basket, breakfast basket, or general cooking baskets. You could also put the items into a large mixing bowl or pot instead of a basket.

Get Well Basket

Fill a basket with items such as books, magazines, tea, candles, soup, mug, straws, and flowers. You can make these for women, men, and children as well.

Muffin Mix Basket

Fill a basket with muffin tins, wooden spoons, a mixing bowl, whisk, and muffin mix. The mix can be store-bought or homemade. If it is homemade, include the recipe.

Homemade Cookie Gifts

Fill a jar with all the dry ingredients used in a cookie recipe. Layer them neatly in the jar and seal tightly. Attach the recipe to the jar with a decorative ribbon. Add a label if desired.

Men's Gift Basket

Start with a bucket or tool belt and fill with items such as tape measures, hammers, hand cleaner, and other small tools or accessories.

Mechanic's Gift Basket

Go down the automotive aisle to get ideas of things to stuff in this basket. You can add shop rags, car wax, sponges, or different car accessories to this basket or bucket.

Sports Fan Basket

Use their favorite team's memorabilia to add to the basket. Add snacks for a game watching party. Pretzels, chips, dips, popcorn, nuts, and drinks are all ideas for this basket.

Pampering Basket

Fill a basket with things to pamper someone. Start with bath beads, bubble bath, candles, lotions, body wash, a bath pillow, a favorite magazine, flavored tea, and chocolate.

New Pet Owner

Go down the pet aisle and fill a basket with pet accessories. Start with a feed bowl, chew toys, bones, treats, pet brushes, shampoo, collars, and canned food.

Family Calendars

A wonderful Christmas gift for grandparents is to take 12 pictures of family members and make a calendar for the following year. This will take some time, but they love it. The best advice I can give is to start this project early!

Coupon Books

Make a nice coupon book for someone who could use your services. Include services such as free babysitting, yard work, house cleaning, errands...

Movie Basket

Fill a basket or bucket with items such as microwave popcorn, soft drinks, candy, movie tickets, videos, or DVDs.

For the Tea Lover

Get a pretty teacup and saucer and fill it with a variety of teas, hot chocolate, candy, cookies, or other small gifts. Wrap it with cellophane and tie a ribbon around the top.

Stationary Set

Fill a basket with cards, stationary, pens, markers, stickers, and don't forget the postage. This would especially be nice for someone who might be moving away. In that case, an address book could be added with names and addresses already filled in of friends and family members.

- Ideas for gift baskets are endless. Decide on a theme or find out what the recipient likes and start filling!

Keeping Your
Household Organized

Her husband has full confidence in her
And lacks nothing of value.
Proverbs 31:11

File it, Don't Pile it!

One of the best techniques I have found for getting rid of piles of paperwork, I got from Emilie Barnes. I keep **3 file folders** close when I go through the mail. One has **Jay's** name on it. Any mail or paperwork he needs to look at goes in this file. The second file says **File It**. This is for all papers waiting to be filed in the filing cabinet. The third file is the **5 Minute** file. These are all things I need to read later or things of action. I may not have time at that particular moment, but will look at later. As you leave to run errands, you can take it with you. Use the time you are waiting in lines or to pick kids up to go through a few items. Every minute counts.

If it is at all possible, get a small filing cabinet and some file folders. Keep everything filed. This keeps the clutter away, but also helps you get to any information you may need. If you cannot get a filing cabinet, use appropriate sized boxes for your filing system.

Storage

If you need to store things in the attic or a storage room, label the boxes. Emilie Barnes has another great idea in this area. After you label the box, number it. Make an index card with that number in the top corner. List all the contents of the box on the card and file the card in a note card file box that is kept in the house. When you need to get something from storage, find the appropriate card with the number. You can go directly to the correct box at this point.

- If you are short on laundry space, get an over the door ironing board. It stays out of the way and folds down as you need it.

- Look at variety stores for storage ideas. There are so many items available today. Pull out baskets, lazy-susans, and portable shelves are just a few that are very helpful.

Organizing Tips

- One way of organizing recipes you cut out of magazines is to put them in a photo album and keep them sorted by categories. This makes it easy to add new recipes and you can still take the recipes out to see the back.

- Keep a planner. In my planner, I have calendars by the month, a place for addresses, places for notes or lists, a notepad, a zipper bag for receipts, and my prayer list by days. I try to never leave the house without my planner. This has been the most help in getting myself organized. A PDA is just as helpful for some people. I just prefer to be able to see all of it at a glance.

- When you receive large restaurant or department store coupons, write the expiration dates down in your planner. Do the same thing for gift certificates.

- Keep lists of things to do each day, people to call, things needed from the store, and errands to run. I also keep these lists in my planner. If I have a few extra minutes during lunch, I can look at the list and get something marked off.

- Keep a weekly calendar with events posted somewhere for the entire family to refer to. Each person can add to the calendar as needed. Everyone can be aware of the events of the week.

- It is a good idea to keep a record of your family's information in one place. Include on this chart, each person, any allergies, dates of shots, birthdays, Christian birthdays, and blood types. In the past, I have had to fill out paperwork for the kids to go to camp. I had to look in several different places to get the correct information.

- I have one chart that has only birthdays and anniversaries of family and close friends on it. The chart is listed by months, so you are less likely to forget an important occasion. (I have included my chart in the Appendix as an example, as well as a blank one).

- I also keep a file folder for each family member in the filing cabinet. Each one contains the same information as the chart mentioned above, but it also includes the actual shot records, birth certificates, and vision prescriptions.

- Keep your closet organized by hanging all hangers in the same direction. Also, hang like items together: skirts, shirts, pants, dresses…

- When you take clothes off of the hangers, put the hangers together in one area. When you get ready to take the hangers to the laundry area, you won't have to go through the entire closet searching for them.

- Save all store receipts. You never know when you will need to return something. If you buy trees or perennials at Wal-Mart or Home Depot, they will replace them or give you your money back if they die within a year. You must have the receipt. Keep all receipts for the year in a file folder with dividers categorizing the receipts for easy access.

- If you itemize on your taxes, keep a spreadsheet of all tax deductible expenses throughout the year. After you enter the receipt, put the receipt in an envelope to have available while figuring your taxes.

For more suggestions, get Emilie Barnes' books, <u>More Hours in My Day</u>, or <u>Creative Home Organizer</u>. They are filled with ideas to help you keep an organized home.

Entertaining & Serving

She gets up while it is still dark;
She provides food for her family
And portions for her servant girls.
Proverbs 31:15

She opens her arms to the poor
And extends her hands to the needy.
Proverbs 31:20

Think of your house, not as yours alone, but as God's gift to you to share with others. Not everyone has the gift of hospitality. However, everyone can make people feel welcome and comfortable in their home.

When you have guests over, you do not have to have elaborate plans or food. Serve simple things so you can visit with your guests instead of having to worry about the food the entire time. Do things that put you and your guests at ease. Remember, it isn't about the plans, the house, or the food. It is about the people you are serving!

Planning a Party

Planning and having a party does not have to be a stressful event. The more organized you are, the less stress you will encounter. To help you stay organized, keep lists for each aspect of the party. For example, start with basic ideas for the menu, theme, decorations, music, activities or games, and of course a "To Do" list.

Basic Decisions:

- Decide on a **date and time** for the party.

- Write out a **guest list**. Make sure all guests are compatible. Consider ages and interests. Your guests should feel very comfortable at the party.

- Decide how **informal or formal** the occasion will be. In doing this, you will be able to better plan the type of food and serving to be done.
  Examples:
  Cookout – Usually on the grill, can be served indoors or outside
  Picnic – Outdoor eating
  Pool Party – Food Outside
  Potluck Dinner – Everyone brings a dish
  Buffet – All food is in one area and guests serve their own plates
  Family Style – All food is on the table
  Formal Sit-Down – Guests sit down and their plates are filled and served

- Decide on a **theme**, if any. Deciding on a theme will direct you in all the other areas. For example, if you decided to have a Hawaiian Luau, your menu, decorations, music... will be directed toward Hawaii. Although a theme can help you in planning, all parties do not require a specific theme.

After these areas have been decided on, go ahead and send out the invitations. Invitations need to be sent out approximately 2 weeks in advance. Include date, time, place, special occasion if any, type of dress if any, and add an RSVP with a phone number. These are very important in knowing how many people to plan for.

Another option is to call each person and invite them to join you personally. If you do make phone calls, use the opportunity to find out if they have any food allergies or diabetic concerns. This will also help you in planning the menu.

Food for the Party:

After you have decided what to serve, you need to do a quick assessment of yourself. Take into consideration your cooking skills and the time you have available to prepare the food. If either of these areas come up short, look for options such as take-out, a caterer, or the deli section of your local grocery store. Nothing says you have to do all of the cooking for any event.

Look at each food item and see which ones can be prepared in advance. Try to have the majority completed and either kept in the refrigerator or frozen a day or two ahead of time. If you try to get all the food cooked on the day of the party, you will most likely go into the party very stressed out.

Supplies:

Several days before the party, check all supplies to make sure you have plenty. You will need chairs, dishes, serving trays and bowls, napkins, cups or glasses, silverware, table cloths, etc. If you need more items, renting is an option. However, I would try to borrow from friends or family members first. Depending on how informal the occasion may be, you may choose to use paper products.

Decorations:

Decorating for a party can be very enjoyable. Dig down deep and use your imagination. Of course candles, streamers, and balloons are always good ways to decorate. However, you can think of so much more to do with table settings if you put your mind to it. Let nature do the decorating for you. Walk out into your yard and find fresh flowers, branches, leaves, nuts, and grasses. Use them in arrangements, loose on the table, or as napkin rings.

Place cards can also be used with the décor. These can be anything that can be personalized. A few ideas are terra cotta pots, any type of note card, cookies, picture frames, votive candles, or small pinecones or artichokes with name cards in them. Again, think about the theme and use what you have.

Time Needed:

Make a schedule for the week of the party to ensure that you end up with enough time to get everything completed early. Set aside time for:

Cleaning
Shopping
Decorating
Cooking
Setting Places
Getting Yourself Dressed and Ready
Relaxing

Entertaining & Serving Tips

- When setting food out for a buffet style party, make cards with labels for each dish so guests will know exactly what they are getting.

- If at all possible, try not to prepare a new recipe for a party. Either try it out beforehand, or use recipes you already know.

- When new families move into the neighborhood, welcome them with an easy dessert. You can use a disposable pan, or put an address label on the bottom of the dish you take. This makes it easy for them to return your dish, and it gives you an opportunity to invite them into your home for another visit.

- Another way of blessing people with hospitality in the way of food is if you are on the receiving end of the dish. As you return the dish to the owner, make sure it is filled with a dessert or casserole. It will truly be a surprised blessing for them.

- Always try to serve people when they are feeling sick. This can be done in many ways. You can fix a meal for their family, run errands for them, baby-sit, or do some sort of chores for them. Cards and phone calls will also do wonders. It is great just to know people are thinking about you.

- Keep a box of greeting cards for all occasions. I have them divided into categories, based on occasions. As the need arrives, you always have an appropriate card.

- Keep a guest register book in your entryway. Have your guests sign as they come to visit. It is neat to look back through the guests who have visited in past years.

- If you are invited to a party, always RSVP in a timely manner. The hostess may need an accurate number so she will know how much food to prepare. Remember that RSVP is to let them know either way, not just if you are coming.

Offer hospitality to one another without grumbling.
I Peter 4:9

Share with God's people who are in need. Practice hospitality.
Romans 12:13

Cooking & Dining

She is like the merchant ships,
Bringing her food from afar.
She gets up while it is still dark;
She provides food for her family
And portions for her servant girls.
Proverbs 31:14,15

While preparing the meal, set the table and get your family ready to pray and eat together. You can have some calm music going, but turn the TV off. Every now and then it is OK to eat in the den in front of the TV, but make eating at the table the norm.

Because you have your family at the table, conversations are more apt to start. You are able to find out what is going on in their lives, and show interest in them. All meal conversations should be pleasant! No arguing or discussing stressful situations at this time.

You do not have to save your best china for company. Pull it out occasionally for your family. Make meal time special and your family will feel just as important as company.

An idea I got from Emilie Barnes was to have a special plate to honor a family member on special occasions. She mentioned having a red plate with some inscription on it. I actually found a red plate that says, "God Thinks You Are Special Today… and Everyday". I pull it out for birthdays, Christian birthdays, special events, or accomplishments. The kids always help me with the setting the table, and they really enjoy the days they get to secretly put out the red plate.

Meal Planning

With so many fads and diet plans going around, it is sometimes hard to tell what is really nutritious. Before jumping into a new diet plan, investigate how healthy and beneficial it truly is. Daily meal planning should consist of the basic food groups: breads & cereals, fruits & vegetables, meats or proteins, and dairy products.

The government recently changed what we have known as the Food Pyramid. It is now called, My Pyramid, allowing people to use it on a more personal level. The pyramid now takes into consideration the age of a person and gives 12 different models that suggest exercise and limiting calorie intake. For a better explanation and a look at the individual models, go to www.mypyramid.com.

Basic Guidelines Offered

Fat-free or lowfat milk – 3 Cups
Fruits – 2 Cups
Vegetables – 2 ½ Cups
3 oz. Of Whole-Grain Foods
As little trans-fatty acid as possible
Less than 1 teaspoon of salt

Cooking and Dining Tips

- When buying lemons, buy them in bulk, by the bag instead of individually. This is much more economical. Unless you plan on using them soon, cut them into quarters and freeze them on a cookie sheet. After they are frozen, place them in a freezer bag and used them as needed.

- Before throwing out orange or lemon rinds, grate them and store in the freezer. You will have already prepared zest for any recipe.

- Watch lots of cooking shows to get tips, ideas, and recipes for future use.

- Watch your local paper for recipes, cooking tips, and upcoming events.

- Attend local cooking classes.

- Magazines can be an excellent source for new recipes. I always carry a notepad and pen with me. If I have to wait at a doctor's office, I have plenty of time to copy recipes that catch my attention. If you run out of time, many offices will copy the recipes for you, or let you cut them out.

- Don't feel guilty about taking shortcuts. There is nothing wrong with using already prepared food.

- To save money on lunchmeat, buy in bulk. At most places, you can take a large ham or piece of bologna to the deli and they will slice it for you for no charge.

- To save time when baking cookies, line cookie sheets with foil before adding cookie dough. When the cookies are finished, remove the foil and replace with another sheet and you are ready for another batch.

- When making a homemade piecrust, roll it out between 2 pieces of waxed paper. It rolls easier and is a lot less mess.

- Piecrusts will be better if you use very cold ingredients. Also, mix only until the ingredients are blended. Too much mixing will cause the dough to be tough.

- Chill pie crust dough before rolling it out. To make it extra flaky, brush the top crust lightly with cold water before baking.

- When making meringue, use egg whites at room temperature. Beat the egg whites until they are stiff before adding the sugar. Use super-fine sugar, a little at a time to keep the meringue from forming the "tears" on the top.

- An easy way to have fresh pies all year is to prepare extra pie fillings. Place them in a foil-lined pie pan and freeze them. Once they are frozen to the shape of the pan, take them out and put into a freezer bag. When you get ready for a pie, bake the crust, add the filling and let it thaw.

- Unless you know you will eat leftovers soon, don't put them in the refrigerator. Instead, put them in individual TV dinner trays and freeze them for a quick meal. Be sure to label what the dish is and the date.

- Freeze raw or cooked meatballs on a cookie sheet. After they are completely frozen, put them into a freezer bag. This will keep them from sticking together. When you are ready for them, you can use as many as you want.

- If you have extra pancake or waffle batter, go ahead and make the extras. You can freeze them and use as needed. Just put them in the microwave for a few seconds until warm.

- For iced drinks, try freezing juice, tea, or fruit in ice trays. Use these instead of ice to keep your drinks from getting watered down.

- Before preparing a casserole to freeze, line the dish with heavy-duty aluminum foil. After the dish is frozen, remove the contents and wrap with another layer of aluminum foil. This keeps your casserole from getting freezer burned, and lets you continue to use your baking dish.

- Before you start cooking, run a sink of dishwater, and make sure the dishwasher is free of clean dishes. Clean as you go. Load the dishwasher as you can, put any dishes that need to soak or will not fit in the dishwasher in the water, and throw all trash away while you cook.

- When you get home with fresh fruits and vegetables, go ahead and wash all of them. Any vegetables that will be chopped up in advance can be chopped up at the same time and stored in the refrigerator. They will be ready when you need them.

- When using nonstick cookware, always use plastic or wooden utensils to keep from scratching the surface.

- Never drain grease into your sink. Always uses a coffee can or other disposable container.

- When sautéing, always heat the skillet for a minute or two before adding the oil. The food will stick less.

- To get more juice out of a lemon, either roll it with the palm of your hand on the counter or microwave it for about 20-30 seconds.

- When cooking a roast, don't salt it until it is almost finished. This will keep the juices from escaping the meat.

- Whipping cream will beat faster if you chill the beater and the bowl in the freezer beforehand.

- When beating whipping cream, add powdered sugar instead of granulated sugar. The texture stays firm longer and does not get watery.

- Always keep the basic foods and staples in your pantry.

- Use a crockpot when you get a chance. On most Sundays, I will put things on to cook when we leave for church. When we get home, it is ready.

- If you are working with a cake that will have some sort of topping that could make a mess on the cake plate, such as dusting with powdered sugar, lay strips of waxed paper around the edges of the cake plate before placing the cake on it. After the cake is decorated, the waxed paper slips right out, and the cake plate is clean.

- Use a plastic cutting board instead of a wooden one when working with meat.

- Unless a recipe states otherwise, mix dry ingredients together before adding liquids, fats, or eggs.

- Always clean your countertops with a disinfectant after working with meats, especially chicken. Bleach and water will kill any salmonella germs. Also, wash your hands after handling the meat.

- I keep a spreadsheet with all the meals we enjoy. They are listed in categories (chicken, pork, beef...). A copy can be found in the Appendix.

- The best way to get the meat out of an avocado is to slice the avocado long ways, all the way around. The knife needs to make a full circle and also needs to cut all the way down to the seed. Twist the 2 halves apart. Thrust the knife into the seed and twist to pop the seed out. With a spoon, scrape the avocado meat out of the shells.

- To mash an avocado up easily, use a pastry blender.

- If you don't like the mess of mixing a meatloaf with your bare hands, put all the ingredients in a large freezer bag and mix.

- Once you have thawed meat out, go ahead and use it. Do not refreeze it.

Basic Kitchen Items

Liquid Measuring Cups
Wooden or Metal Spoons
Timer
Colander
Skillet
Mixing Bowls
Whisk
Pans
Pyrex Dishes
Kitchen Scissors

Measuring Spoons
Spatulas
Tongs
Good Knives
Dutch Oven
Cake Pans
Cookie Sheets
Can Opener
Recipe Books
Plastic Cutting Board

Staples to Have on Hand

Flour
Salt
Eggs
Spices (Your favorites)
Tea Bags
Baking Powder

Sugar
Pepper
Milk
Vegetable Oil
Baking Soda
Vanilla

Small Appliances

Crockpot
Electric Skillet
Food Processor
Blender
Waffle Iron
Breadmaker
Food Dehydrator

Coffee Pot
Toaster
Deep Fryer
Mixer (Hand or Stand)
Ice Cream Maker
Juicer

Cooking Terms

Baste: To spoon liquid or fat over food while it is cooking to prevent it from drying out.

Blanch: To immerse in boiling water for a brief time and then into cold water.

Deep Fry: To submerge food, usually with a batter, in a large pan of heated oil.

Fold: To combine ingredients with a delicate mixture, such as egg whites or whipped cream, without losing the air. You gently put a spatula down into the center of the mixture, across the bottom of the bowl, and back over to the top, "folding" until it is mixed evenly.

Fry: To cook in a skillet with oil.

Julienne: To cut food into long, thin strips.

Marinate: To let something set in a liquid for a period of time to make it more flavorful and tender.

Sauté: To cook in a skillet in a small amount of shortening, until it is tender.

Scald: To heat something, just below the boiling point.

Score: To cut shallow lines, usually diamond shaped, into food before cooking.

Sear: To put a quick, high heat on food, to brown just the surface of the food.

Simmer: To cook in liquid, just below the boiling point so that there are tiny bubbles in the pan.

Steam: To cook over boiling water, usually in a steamer basket, with a lid on the pan. The food is not in water.

Stew: To cook in liquid very slowly and for an extended period of time.

Stock: The liquid in which meat or vegetables have been cooked.

Whisk: A wire instrument used for hand beating.

Cooking terms were taken from <u>Pillsbury Kitchens' Cookbook</u>, 1984.

Cooking Measurements

3 teaspoons = 1 Tablespoon
2 Tablespoons =1 fluid oz.
1 fluid oz. = 1/8 Cup
4 Tablespoons = ¼ Cup
1 Cup = 8 fluid oz.
2 Cups = 1 pint = 16 oz.
2 Pints = 1 quart = 32 oz.
4 Cups = 1 quart
4 Quarts = 1 Gallon
16 oz. = 1 lb.

Cooking Substitutions

1 Cup **Buttermilk** = 1 Tablespoon vinegar or lemon juice plus milk to make 1 Cup

1 Square (1 oz.) **Unsweetened Chocolate** = 3 Tablespoons unsweetened cocoa + 1 Tablespoon shortening or margarine

2 oz. **Semi-Sweet Chocolate** = 1/3 Cup semi-sweet chocolate chips

½ Cup **Corn Syrup** = ½ Cup sugar + 2 Tablespoons of liquid

1 Cup **Heavy Cream** (for baking, not whipping) = ¾ Cup whole milk + ¼ Cup butter

1 Cup **Cake Flour** = 7/8 Cups all-purpose flour + 2 Tablespoons cornstarch

1 **Garlic Clove** = 1/8 teaspoon minced garlic or garlic powder or ½ teaspoon garlic salt

1 Tablespoon **Fresh Herbs** = 1 teaspoon dried herbs

1 Cup **Honey** = 1 ¼ Cup sugar + ¼ Cup liquid

1 Cup Whole Milk = ½ evaporated milk + ½ Cup water

Recipes for Your Family

Better a meal of vegetables where there is love than a
fattened calf with hatred.
Proverbs 15:17

So whether you eat or drink or whatever you do, do it all
for the glory of God.
I Corinthians 10:31

Desserts

- Peach Cobbler
- Cold Oven Pound Cake
- Caramel Graham Cracker Cookies
- Reesies
- Creamy Banana Pudding
- Quick Shortbread Cookies
- Peanut Butter Clusters
- Coconut Macaroons

Main Dishes

- Hot Sauce Chicken
- Meatloaf
- Chicken Spaghetti
- Baked Fish
- Pork Loin with Vegetables
- Spanish Chicken & Rice
- Swiss Cilantro Chicken
- Italian Parmesan Chicken
- Parmesan Fried Chicken

Vegetables and Side Dishes

- Corn Casserole
- Green Bean Casserole
- Cheesy Potatoes
- Mashed Potatoes
- Grilled or Baked Garden Vegetables
- Homemade Macaroni and Cheese
- Guacamole

Soups

- Taco Soup
- Cheesy Chicken Noodle Soup
- Tortilla Soup
- Tomato Basil Bisque
- Potato Soup
- Stew

Canning

- Dill Pickles
- Jalepeno Peppers
- Dried Beans
- Sliced Peaches
- Cherries
- Plums

Breads

- Butter Bud Biscuits
- Monkey Bread
- Easy Dinner Rolls
- Hush Puppies
- Cornbread
- Pizza Bread
- Pumpkin Muffins

Desserts

Peach Cobbler

1 Large Can of Sliced Peaches in Heavy Syrup
½ Cup of Water
1 White or Yellow Cake Mix
1 Stick of Margarine or Butter
Cinnamon to top

Directions: Spray a 9 ½ X 13 casserole dish with Pam. Empty the can of peaches into the dish. Add water. Spread the dry cake mix on top of the peaches. Cut pats of butter and place them on the cake mix. Top with cinnamon. Bake at 350 for approximately 30 minutes, until brown.

(Recipe by Dawn White)

Cold Oven Pound Cake

3 Sticks of Margarine or Butter
1 - 8 oz. Package of Cream Cheese
3 Cups of Sugar
3 Cups of Sifted Flour
6 Eggs
2 Teaspoons of vanilla

Directions: Cream butter, cream cheese, and sugar well. Add eggs 1 at a time, beating well after each addition. Next, add flour and vanilla. Beat well. Place in a well greased tube pan.

Bake in a cold oven (not preheated) at 300 for 2 hours.

• If you want to add nuts, cherries, coconut, or other ingredients, you can.
(Recipe by Kathy Jobe)

Caramel Graham Cracker Cookies

2 Sticks of Real Butter
1 Cup of Brown Sugar
Graham Crackers
Chopped Nuts

Directions: Preheat oven to 350. Line cookie sheet with foil. Spray with Pam. Lay graham crackers out as closely as you can. Spread chopped nuts on top.

Melt butter in a saucepan. Add brown sugar. Bring to a boil. Boil exactly 3 minutes. Pour over the crackers and nuts. Bake at 350 for 8 minutes. Cool.

(Recipe by Merlyn Rivers)

Reesies

2 Sticks of Melted Butter or Margarine
1 ½ Cups of Graham Cracker Crumbs
1 Box of Powdered Sugar
1 Cup of Peanut Butter
2 Tablespoons of Shortening
12 oz. Package of Semi-Sweet Chocolate Chips

Directions:

Combine margarine, graham cracker crumbs, powdered sugar, and peanut butter. Then press into a 9" X 13" pan. Mix together in saucepan the shortening and chocolate chips over low heat, stirring constantly until melted and smooth. Pour over the graham cracker mixture and allow to cool completely. Cut into squares. Best if kept in the refrigerator.

Creamy Banana Pudding

1 (14 oz.) Can of Eagle Brand Milk
1 ½ Cup of Cold Water
1 (3 ½ oz.) Package of Vanilla Pudding & Pie Filling Mix
2 Cups (1 Pint) Whipping Cream – Whipped in a very cold bowl
36 Vanilla Wafers
3 Medium Bananas

Directions:

Combine Eagle Brand Milk and Water and mix well. Add pudding mix and beat with an electric mixer until well blended. Chill for 5 minutes. Fold in Whipped Cream.

In a bowl or Pyrex dish, layer cookies, bananas, pudding, several times. End with either pudding or cookies. Chill for at least 3 hours.

Quick Shortbread Cookies

1 1/8 Cup of Butter or Margarine
5/8 Cup of Sugar
2 ¼ Cup of Sifted Flour
1 Teaspoon of Vanilla
Powdered Sugar

Directions:

Mix all ingredients well and roll into small balls. Flatten with fingers onto a cookie sheet. Bake at 350 degrees for 10-12 minutes. As soon as you take them out, sprinkle them with powdered sugar.

Peanut Clusters

1 (16 oz.) Package of Semi-Sweet Chocolate Chips
1 Package of Peanut Butter Chips
1 Jar of Dry Roasted Peanuts

Directions:

In a large bowl, melt both packages of Chips in the microwave. Stir in the jar of peanuts and mix well. Drop by spoonfuls onto waxed paper and let set. To speed up the setting process, put them in the refrigerator.

(Recipe by Rhonda Kimble)

Coconut Macaroons

2 2/3 Cups of Coconut
2/3 Cups of Eagle Brand Sweetened Condensed Milk
1 Teaspoon of Vanilla

Directions:

Mix all ingredients well. Drop by teaspoons, 1 inch apart onto a well-greased baking sheet. Bake at 350 degrees for 8-10 minutes or until lightly browned. Remove at once from baking sheet.

(Recipe by Linda Sikes)

Main Dishes

Hot Sauce Chicken

Boneless Skinless Chicken
Picante Sauce of your Choosing
3-4 Tablespoons of Butter or Margarine
Salt & Pepper
Grated Cheddar Cheese

Directions:

Preheat the oven to 400 degrees. Put butter in a Pyrex dish and melt it in the oven. Salt and Pepper both sides of the chicken and place it in the melted butter. Cover each piece of chicken in Picante Sauce. Bake in the oven for 45 minutes. During the last 5 minutes of the cooking time, sprinkle grated cheese on top of each piece of chicken and let it melt.

Old-Fashioned Meatloaf

1 ½ -2 lbs. of Ground Beef
1 (12oz.) Can of Tomato Sauce
Salt & Pepper to Your Taste
1 ½ Cups of Diced Vegetables (Onions, Bell Peppers) Frozen Foods Section
1 Roll of Ritz Crackers – Crumbled into fine pieces
2 Eggs
1 Cup of Ketchup
½ Cup of Water

Preheat oven to 350 degrees. Spray a baking dish with Pam. Mix 1st 6 ingredients together well. The best way is to use your hands. Press the mixture into the baking dish. Bake for about 45 minutes. Mix the ketchup with the water and spread on top of the meatloaf. Bake another 10 minutes.

You can also make individual meatloaves in muffin tins. These will cook in about ½ the amount of time.

Chicken Spaghetti

1 Package of Angel Hair Pasta or Spaghetti
1 Family Size Can of Cream of Mushroom Soup
1 Cup of Chicken Broth
3 Tablespoons of Margarine
2 Cans of Chicken
2 Cups of Grated Cheddar Cheese
1 Can of Mushrooms Drained (optional)

Directions:

In a dutch oven, boil pasta for the recommended time on the package. Drain the noodles in a colander and leave in the sink until needed later. Mix margarine, mushroom soup, broth, chicken and mushrooms in the same dutch oven and heat over medium heat until mixed well and warm. Add the pasta back into the chicken mixture and stir well. Place ingredients in a baking dish that has been sprayed with Pam. Top the casserole with grated cheese and bake at 350 degrees until the cheese is completely melted and the casserole is bubbly.

Baked Fish

½ Stick of Butter or Margarine
Frozen Fish Fillets
Seasoning Salt
Pepper
Chopped Cilantro (Fresh or Dried)

Directions:

Preheat oven to 400 degrees. Melt butter in a baking dish. Place fish in butter and season generously with seasoning salt, pepper, and cilantro on both sides. Bake for approximately 45 minutes.

Pork Loin with Vegetables

1 Pork Tenderloin
4 Bell Peppers
1 Purple Onion
3 Tomatoes
3 Fresh Jalepenos
Seasoning Salt
Pepper
Olive Oil

Directions:

Preheat oven to 375 degrees. Line a cookie sheet or baking dish with foil. Cut the pork loin into 3 inch long pieces. Place the pork loin pieces on the foil and season with seasoning salt and pepper generously. Cut all vegetables in large chunks and place on top of the pork loin. Drizzle olive oil over the meal, cover with foil, and bake for approximately 1 hour.

Spanish Chicken & Rice

2 Packages of Lipton Spanish Rice
4 Tablespoons of Butter or Margarine
3 Cups of Water
1 Cup of Picante Sauce
Boneless Skinless Chicken (equivalent of 6-8 Breasts)
2 Cups of Grated Cheddar Cheese

Directions:

In a crockpot, mix 1st 4 ingredients together. Push chicken pieces down into the rice mixture and cook on high heat for 3-4 hours. Lengthen the time if the chicken is frozen. Sprinkle Cheese on top and cook until the cheese is melted.

Cilantro Chicken

Boneless Skinless Chicken Pieces
1 Can of Rotel Tomatoes
1 Onion, Sliced
Cilantro
Margarine

Directions:

Place chicken pieces in baking dish. Season with salt & pepper. Cover with Rotel tomatoes, onion, and desired amount of cilantro. Dot with margarine. Bake at 350 for 50 minutes. Serve with rice.

Italian Parmesan Chicken

Boneless Skinless Chicken Pieces
Parmesan Cheese
1 Large Can of Spaghetti Sauce
Spaghetti

Directions:

Place chicken pieces in a baking dish. Season with salt & pepper. Cover with spaghetti sauce and bake at 350 for 40 minutes. Cover with Parmesan Cheese and bake until the cheese is melted. Serve over spaghetti.

Parmesan Fried Chicken

Boneless Skinless Chicken Pieces
Shredded Parmesan Cheese

Directions:

Coat chicken pieces with Parmesan Cheese. Use enough oil to coat the bottom of a nonstick skillet. Fry chicken in hot oil.

Vegetables & Side Dishes

Corn Casserole

1 Can of Whole Corn
1 Can of Cream Style Corn
1 Individual Package of Cornbread Mix
1 Cup of Sour Cream
1 Stick of Melted Butter or Margarine

Directions:

Preheat oven to 350 degrees. Mix all ingredients and pour into a greased baking dish. Bake until firm, approximately 30-45 minutes.

(Recipe by Grace Chapman)

Green Bean Casserole

2 Cans of Green Beans, Drained
¾ Cups of Milk
1 Can of Cream of Mushroom Soup
Salt & Pepper to Taste
1 Can of French Fried Onions

Directions:

Combine all ingredients with ½ of the onions. Pour into a greased baking dish. Bake at 350 degrees for 30 minutes. Top with the remaining onions and bake another 5 minutes longer.

Cheesy Potatoes

1 Stick of Butter or Margarine
6-7 Medium Baking Potatoes
Salt & Pepper to Taste
½ Cup of Heavy Cream
1 Lb. Of Velveeta Cheese

Directions:

Peel potatoes and boil until tender, approximately 30 minutes. Drain water and cut potatoes into cubes. In a large saucepan, mix all remaining ingredients and cook on low heat until cheese is melted and the mixture is smooth. Pour over the potatoes and serve.

Mashed Potatoes

6-7 Medium Baking Potatoes
1 ½ Sticks of Butter or Margarine
¼ - ½ Cups of Heavy Cream
Salt & Pepper to Taste

Directions:

Peel and boil potatoes. Put potatoes, butter, salt & pepper into a large mixing bowl and beat. Add cream to get to the desired consistency.

Baked Garden Vegetables

Salt & Pepper
Olive Oil
Zucchini
Purple Onion
Squash
Bell Peppers
Jalepeno Peppers
Tomatoes
Mushrooms
(Almost any vegetables can be used)

Directions:

Wash and cut all vegetables into chunks. On a foil covered baking sheet, lay vegetables out and drizzle with olive oil and seasonings. Cover with foil and bake at 350 degrees for approximately 20 minutes or until tender.

Homemade Macaroni and Cheese

1 Large Bag of Elbow Macaroni
¼ Cup of Butter or Margarine
1 Cup of Buttermilk
2 Lbs. Of Velveeta Cheese

Directions:

In a large dutch oven, boil macaroni according the package directions. Drain and leave in the colander until ready to add back to the cheese mixture. In the same dutch oven, cut Velveeta into small cubes, add buttermilk, and butter. Melt over medium low heat until it is completely smooth. Add the macaroni into the cheese mixture and salt to taste.

(Recipe by Jay Sikes)

Guacamole

2 ripened Avocados
About 1/3 C. Picante Sauce of your choice
Garlic Powder
Salt & Pepper
1 T. Lemon Juice
Jalepeno Salt (if desired)

Directions:

Put avocado meat in a bowl and mash with a fork or a pastry blender. Add all other ingredients to taste. Stir well and refrigerate until ready to serve.

Soups

Taco Soup

2 Lbs. Hamburger Meat
1 Medium Onion - Chopped
1 Package Dry Ranch Dressing
1 Package Taco Seasoning
1 Can of Corn – Drained
2 Cans of Rotel Tomatoes
1 Large Can of Crushed Tomatoes
1 Can of Ranch Style Pinto Beans
1 Can of Pinto Beans with Jalepeno Peppers (optional)
4 Cups of Water
1 ½ Lb. Velveeta Cheese – cut into cubes

Directions:

Brown ground beef and onion in a large dutch oven. Drain the fat off of the meat. Add all ingredients except the cheese to the pan and simmer until thoroughly heated. Before serving, add the cubes of cheese and warm while stirring until completely melted.
(Recipe from Patsy Leshe)

Cheesy Chicken Noodle Soup

2 Large Cans of Progresso Chicken Noodle Soup
1 Can of Chicken Broth
1 Can of Chicken
½ Lb. Of Velveeta Cheese

Directions:

Warm all ingredients over medium heat. Once warm, add Velveeta Cheese until melted. Serve hot.

Tortilla Soup

1 Large Can of Chicken & Rice Soup
½ Cup of Hot Sauce
½ Cup of Water
Cilantro to Taste
1 Can of Chicken
Tortilla Chips
Grated Mozzarella Cheese to Garnish

Directions:

Add all ingredients together except tortillas and cheese. Cook on stovetop on medium heat. When completely heated, pour over crumbled tortilla chips and top with cheese.

Potato Soup

3 Cups of peeled, diced Potatoes
2 Cups of Water
1 Teaspoon of Salt
1 Chopped Onion
3 Tablespoons of Butter or Margarine
2 Tablespoons of Flour
2 Cups of Milk
1 Teaspoon of Dried Parsley
½ Teaspoon of Garlic Powder
1 Teaspoon of Pepper

Directions:

Bring potatoes, water, and salt to a boil in a saucepan. Reduce heat and simmer, covered, for 15 minutes or until the potatoes are tender. Without draining the potatoes, slightly mash them up.

In a separate saucepan, melt the butter and add onion. Sauté until the onion is soft. Sprinkle in the flour and stir for one minute. Gradually add the milk, stirring frequently for 5-10 minutes or until thick. Add cooked potato mixture and seasonings. Mix well.

Tomato Basil Bisque

4 Cups of Tomato Juice
4 Cans of Diced Tomatoes
1 Cup of Heavy Whipping Cream
12 Freshly Chopped Basil Leaves
½ Cup of Sweet Butter, Softened
½ Teaspoon of Ground Pepper

Directions:

Mix tomatoes and juice in a saucepan and simmer for 30 minutes over a medium-low heat. Cool slightly, then place in a blender or food processor. Add basil and process more. You may have to do this in batches. Place the mixture back into the pan and add cream and butter. Continue stirring until blended well. Add salt and pepper to taste. Serve hot. If desired, garnish with more basil or Parmesan cheese.

Stew

2 Lbs. Of Your Choice of Beef (Ground beef, Stew Meat, Round Steak)
1 Large Onion
2 Cans of Diced Potatoes or 2 Medium Potatoes (Peeled and Diced)
1 Can of Carrots or 3-4 Carrots (Peeled and Diced)
1 Can of Green Beans
1 Can of Whole Corn
1 Can of Rotel Tomatoes
1 (16 oz.) Can of Tomato Sauce
1 Small Bag of Macaroni

Directions:

1- Prepare meat – If using Ground Beef, brown it and drain the fat. Stew Meat is ready to go. Round Steak just needs to be cut into bite-size pieces.
2- Add all ingredients except macaroni, add water to come up about 1-2 inches above all ingredients, and bring to a boil. Season with salt and pepper. Cover and reduce heat. Simmer until all vegetables and tender. Stir periodically to keep from sticking. Add macaroni and boil 10-15 minutes longer. Serve hot.

Canning

Basic Directions:

- Always choose fresh foods.
- Wash all foods thoroughly.
- Store canned foods in a cool, dry place.
- Make sure jars are clean. For pressure canner or boiling bath methods, jars do not have to be sterilized.
- Prepare caps by placing them in a pan and covering with boiling water. Do not boil them, but keep them in the hot water until ready to use.
- Always test the seal: 1-feel to make sure it is down and will not pop up, 2-See that the center of the lid is curved down.
- After food and liquid is in jars, run a butter knife down into the mixture several times to remove any air bubbles.
- Clean the edges of the jars before putting the seals and lids on.

Methods:

Pressure Canner

This method is recommended for processing all Low-Acid Foods. All meats and vegetables except tomatoes and sauerkraut are considered low-acid. This method requires you to follow the manufacturer's instructions for the pressure canner.

Boiling Water Bath

This method is used for tomatoes, fruits, and pickles. These foods have acid in them and can be canned safely with this method.

This method requires a large, deep pan. Place a rack in the bottom of the pan so the jars are not directly on the heated surface of the pan. It should be at least ½ inch from the bottom.   Fill the pan with water and begin to heat the water while you are preparing the food. You need to have enough water to cover the jars at least 1 inch above the tops. It must be boiling before placing the jars into the water.

Place jars on the rack, in the boiling water, leaving enough room in between the jars for good circulation. Make sure the water is 1 inch above the jars, if not, add more boiling water to the pan. Start the timing process as soon as the water returns to a boil. Keep the water boiling the entire time, adding boiling water as needed. As soon as the time is up, remove the jars. Set them upright, 2-3 inches apart. Place them on a cloth to cool. After they have cooled, test the seal. Wash and dry jars before storing.

Reprocessing Jars that Didn't Seal

Check for damaged seals. Replace seals and lids.

Reprocess in Boiling Water Bath for 10 minutes.

Reprocess in Pressure Canner for 1/3 of the original canning time, after the canner has been exhausted for 10 minutes.

(All Canning Recipes by Kerr Glass Manufacturing Corp. unless otherwise stated)

Dill Pickles
(Recipe by Becky Arey)

Fresh Cucumbers
1 or 2 Grape Leaves
1 Garlic Button
1 or 2 Jalepeno Peppers
Sprig of Dill
Pinch of Alum (Very Little!)
6 Cups of Water
2 Cup of Apple Cider Vinegar
1/3 Cup of Plain Salt

Directions:

Wash cucumbers and soak in tap water over night. The next morning, pack cucumbers, grape leaves, garlic, jalepenos, dill, and alum tightly in a gallon jar. Boil the water, salt, and vinegar. While this mixture is heating up, boil the lids to the jar/jars in another pan for 10 minutes. Pour the mixture over the cucumbers. Take the lids directly from the boiling water and seal the jar tightly. Check the lid later. It should not pop when pressure is put on it. If it does, keep the cucumbers in the refrigerator the entire 30 days.

Jalepeno Peppers

Jalepeno Peppers
1 Cup Vinegar
¼ Cup of Water
¼ Cup of Olive Oil
1 Teaspoon of Salt
1 Teaspoon of Pickling Spices

Directions:

Wash peppers. Pack whole or sliced peppers tightly in jars. Boil all other ingredients. Pour over peppers, leaving 1 inch at the top of the jar. Put on caps and screw band firmly tight. Process 10 minutes in a Boiling Water Bath.

Dried Beans (Any Type)

Directions:

Wash beans well, and soak in cold water overnight. Boil beans for 15 minutes. Pack loosely in jars to within 2 inches from the top. Add 1 teaspoon of salt to each quart jar. Fill jar to within ½ of top with precooking water. Put on cap, screw band tightly. Use 10 Pounds of pressure. Cook for 60 minutes.

Syrup for Canned Fruits

1 Cup of Sugar + 3 Cups of Water for **Thin Syrup** (Small, Thin Fruits)
1 Cup of Sugar + 2 Cups of Water for **Medium Syrup** (Peaches, apples,
pears, and sour berries)
1 cup of Sugar + 1 Cup of Water for **Heavy Syrup** (All sour fruits or those
you want to be extra sweet)

Directions:

Make syrup according to the sweetness desired. Boil sugar and water together until
sugar is dissolved. Juice of the fruit may be used in place of water. Keep syrup hot,
but do not let it boil down. Syrup should be boiling when poured over fruits.

Sliced Peaches

Choose ripe firm peaches. Peel and remove the pits. Pack halves or slices into jars to
within ½ inch of the top. Fill to within 1 ½ inches of top of jar with boiling syrup.
Put on cap, and screw band tightly. Use a boiling water bath for 25 minutes.

Cherries

Wash, stem and pit (optional) cherries. Pack into jars to within ½ inch of top. Fill
to within 1 ½ inch of top of jar with boiling syrup. Put on cap, screw lid on tightly.
Use a boiling water bath for 20 minutes.

Plums

Select plums that are not too ripe. Wash and prick skin with needle to prevent
bursting. Pack into jars to within ½ inch of the top. Fill to within
1 ½ inches of top of jar with boiling syrup. Put on cap and screw lid on tightly.
Use a boiling water bath for 25 minutes.

Breads

Butter Bud Biscuits

¼ Cup Margarine
1 ¼ Cup Flour
2 Teaspoons Sugar
2 Teaspoons Baking Powder
1 Teaspoon of Salt
2/3 Cups of Milk

Directions:

Preheat oven to 450 degrees. Mix all dry ingredients together well. Next add the margarine and milk. Form dough into biscuit shapes and onto a baking sheet. Bake until golden brown, about 15-20 minutes.

(Recipe by Joy Chapman)

Monkey Bread

3 Large Cans of Biscuits
½ Cup of Sugar
3 Tablespoons of Cinnamon
1 Stick of Butter or Margarine
1 Teaspoon of Vanilla

Directions:

Mix cinnamon and ½ Cup of sugar together. Melt butter, ½ Cup of sugar, and vanilla together. Cut biscuits into 4 pieces and coat well with the cinnamon/sugar mixture. When you have coated 1 ½ Cans of biscuits, put the biscuits into a greased bundt pan. Pour ½ of the melted butter mixture over the biscuits. Coat the remaining biscuits and put in the bundt pan. Pour the remainder of the butter mixture, and remainder of cinnamon and sugar mixture over them. Bake at 320 degrees for 20-25 minutes.

Easy Dinner Rolls

1 Cup of warm water (105-115 degrees)
2 Packages of Active Dry Yeast
1 Stick of Melted Butter
½ Cup of Sugar
3 Eggs
1 Teaspoon of Salt
4 – 4 ½ Cups Unbleached, All-Purpose Flour
Additional Melted Butter (optional)

Directions:
Combine the warm water and yeast in a large bowl. Let the mixture stand until yeast is foamy, about 5 minutes. Stir in butter, sugar, eggs, and salt. Beat in flour, 1 cup at a time, until dough is too stiff to mix (some flour may not be needed). Cover and refrigerate for 2 hours. (It can be left for up to 4 days at this stage).

Grease a 13 X 9 inch baking pan. Turn the chilled dough out onto a lightly floured board. Divide dough into 24 equal-size pieces. Roll each piece into a smooth round ball. Place balls in even rows in the prepared pan. Cover and let dough balls rise until doubled in volume, about 1 hour.

Preheat oven to 375 degrees. Bake until rolls are golden brown, 15-20 minutes. Brush warm rolls with melted butter, if desired.

Hush Puppies

Vegetable Oil
2 ¼ Cups of Yellow Cornmeal
1 Teaspoon of Salt
2 Tablespoons of Finely Chopped Onion
¾ Teaspoon of Baking Soda
1 ½ Cups of Buttermilk

Directions:
Heat 1 inch of oil in a pan or skillet. Mix dry ingredients. Stir in milk. Drop by spoonfuls into hot oil. Fry until golden brown, about 2 minutes.

Cornbread

1 ½ Cups of Corn Meal
2 Heaping Tablespoons of Flour
1 Teaspoon of Baking Soda
1 Teaspoon of Salt
1 Egg
2 Cups of Buttermilk
¼ Cup of Cooking Oil

Directions:

Preheat oven to 450 degrees. Pour oil into an oven proof skillet and heat in the oven until very hot, approximately 10 minutes. Mix all dry ingredients well, and then add the egg and buttermilk. Mix well. When the oil is heated, pour it into the cornbread mixture. It will sizzle when it is hot enough. Stir it in carefully. When mixed well, pour the mixture back into the skillet and bake for about 30 minutes or until golden brown.

(Recipe by Lester Chapman)

Pizza Bread

1 ½ Cups of Buttermilk Baking Mix
1 Cup of Shredded Cheddar cheese
¾ Cups of Chopped Pepperoni
1 Egg
¼ Cup of Milk
1 Teaspoon of Italian Seasoning

Directions:

Preheat oven to 400 degrees. Grease a 9 inch pie plate. Mix baking mix, ½ cup of the cheese, ½ cup of the pepperoni, the egg, milk, and the seasoning. Spread the mixture in the pie plate. Sprinkle the remaining cheese and pepperoni on top and bake about 20 minutes. A wooden toothpick inserted in the center should come out clean.

Pumpkin Muffins

1 Egg
½ Cup of Milk
½ Cup of Canned Pumpkin
¼ Cup of Melted Butter or Margarine
1 ½ Cups of All-Purpose Flour
½ Cup of Sugar
2 Teaspoons of Baking Powder
½ Teaspoon of Salt
½ Teaspoon of Ground Cinnamon
½ Teaspoon of Ground Nutmeg
½ Cup of Raisins (optional)

Directions:

Preheat oven to 400 degrees. Grease bottoms only of 12 muffin cups. Beat egg well. Stir in milk, pumpkin, margarine, and raisins if desired. After mixed well, stir in remaining ingredients all at once. Stir until flour is moistened – the dough will still be lumpy. Fill muffin cups 2/3 full. Sprinkle ¼ of a teaspoon of sugar over the batter in each cup if desired. Bake for approximately 20 minutes, until golden brown. Remove immediately from the pan.

Other Easy Meals

These require no directions

Corny Dogs with Macaroni and Cheese
Chili Cheese Tator Tots
Tamales with Chili and Cheese
Frozen Burritos/Chimichangas with Chili and Cheese
Hamburger Helper
Stir Fry in the Frozen Foods Section
Frozen Lasagna
Frozen Pizza
Hot Dogs
Frito Chili Pie
Frozen Raviolis with Spaghetti Sauce
Chicken Alfredo (Lipton Alfredo & add 2 Cans of Chicken)
Ground Beef with Ranch Style Beans and Cheddar Cheese

Miscellaneous Household Tips

May the favor of the Lord our God rest upon us;
Establish the work of our hands for us —
Yes, establish the work of our hands.
Psalms 90:17

- Keep a notepad and pen beside your bed, in the bathroom, and in your car. When you think of something you need to take a note of, you can do it right then, before you forget.

- When you go on vacation, have all instructions for mail, newspaper, care of pets, and plant care typed up for the person who will have the responsibility. Save the instructions on the computer or make multiple copies for future use.

- If you don't usually have enough time to read magazines when you first get them, go through and mark the pages that interest you. Keep your magazines in the bathroom, the den (while your family is watching a show you aren't really interested in), the bedroom, and the car. When you have some extra time, read the articles you are most interested in.

- Don't let TV rob you of your time. It is the biggest thief of family time!

- Carry address labels in your purse or planner.

- Eggshells and coffee grounds are great to add to plants. Each day, I throw the coffee grounds into the flowerbed to give a little more nourishment.

- Several years ago as a safety measure against fire, I started keeping all negatives from pictures in my safety deposit box. I kept 1 copy of all studio pictures in there as well. If anything were to happen, I could get them remade.

- I keep all daily make-up items in a zippered bag in the bathroom. First of all, all items are handy and easy to get to. Secondly, when packing to go on a trip, you don't have to worry about leaving something behind. Last of all, there have been times that I was running late and was able to grab the bag and go. I do not recommend doing your make-up while driving, but you will be able to find the time once you get to where you are going.

- If you do not sew, but need something hemmed, use Stitch Witchery. You iron it on. There is no sewing involved.

- To save time and gas, plan to run errands that are in the same area instead of running back and forth.

- If you know you are going to need to take something with you as you leave the house, go ahead and load it in the car or put it in front of the door. If it is something that cannot be left out early, put a note on your purse or in the floor where you will have to walk over it to get to the car.

- If you need to recharge your cell phone before you leave the house, but are afraid you will forget and leave it at home, put the house phone on top of your purse. This will serve as a reminder to switch phones.

- For stings from jellyfish and bees, apply a paste made with meat tenderizer and water. This will take away the sting.

- If your dog needs a pill, put it in bread or meat. I have found that about an inch of a hot dog works perfectly. It slides right in and the dog never knows it is there.

- If your car fits into the garage tightly, hang a tennis ball from the ceiling at the point where you need to stop. When it hits the windshield, you will know you are in the right place.

- When looking for a specific item, call around to stores to see where you can find it before driving around searching for it.

- When available, schedule the first appointments for the day. They are usually on time at that point, and your daytime is not chopped up.

- When scheduling doctor or dental check-ups, try to schedule your appointments as well as your children's appointments with the same office at the same time. This will cut down on trips and waiting times.

- If you use a cell phone, program as many friends', acquaintances', and business phone numbers as you can. This helps if you are out and need to reach someone.

- Keep an extra phone book in the car. On occasion, you will need to call people who are not in your phone register. This helps save time. If you can call in your fast food order, you do not have to wait when you get to the window. Not all restaurants will take call in orders, but it doesn't hurt to ask.

Appendix

And as for you brothers, never tire of doing what is right.
2 Thessalonians 3:13

Appendix Contents

1. Meals Spreadsheet

2. Weekly Menu

3. Generic Shopping List

4. Wal-Mart Shopping List (2 Pages)

5. Household Cleaning Jobs

6. My Personal Birthday Chart

7. Blank Birthday Chart

Chicken

Spanish Ch. & Rice	
Baked Chicken	
Fried Chicken	
Chicken & Rice	
Chicken Pot Pie	
Chicken Spaghetti	
Chicken in its own gravy	
Hot Sauce Chicken	
Chicken & Dumplings	
Chicken Alfredo	
BarBQ Chicken	
Swiss Chicken	
King Ranch Chicken	
Dorito Ch. Casserole	
Chicken Stir Fry	

Pork

Roast	
Pork Chops	
Pork Loin	
Ham	

Beef

Hamburgers	
Tater Tot Casserole	
Chili	
Spaghetti	
Chicken Fried Steak	
Ranch St. Beans & Meat	
Steak	
Salsbury Steak	
Lasagna	
Manicotti	
Meat Pie	
Brisket	
Meatballs	
Meatloaf	
Beef Tips & Rice	
Beef Tips & Noodles	
Pepper Steak	
Goulash	
Hamburger Helper	
Stuffed Bell Peppers	

Seafood

Fish Sticks	
Baked Fish	
Boiled Shrimp	
Grilled Shrimp	
Fried Shrimp	
Fried Fish	
Salmon Patties	
Stuffed Crab	

Breakfast

Waffles	
Pancakes	
Muffins	
Omelets	
Eggs	
Bacon	
Sausage	
Breakfast Casserole	

Miscellaneous Meals

Red beans & Cornbread	
Hot Links	
Hot Dogs	
Corny Dogs	
Frito Pie	
Stew w/ Bisquits	
Frozen Pizza	
Raviolis	
Turkey & Dressing	
Turkey & Rice	
Cheese Dip	
BarBQ Weiners	
Weiners in Croissants	
Tater Tots w/ Chili	

Mexican Food

Chicken Chimichangas	
Fajitas	
Tacos	
Chalupas	
Enchiladas	
Stacked Enchiladas	
Ch. Enchilada Casserole	
Chimichangas	
Burritos	
Taco Salad	
Quesadillas	
Nachos	

Sandwiches

Fried Bologna	
Lunchmeat	
Tuna	

Weekly Menu				Date _____
	Breakfast	Lunch	Dinner	Notes
Monday				
Tuesday				
Wednesday				
Thursday				
Friday				
Saturday				
Sunday				

Shopping List

Qty.	Staples
	Cereal
	Flour
	Sugar
	Oil
	Jell-O
	Mixes
	Nuts
	Stuffing
	G.Cracker Crust
	Coffee
	Creamer
	Chocolate Chips
	Coconut

Qty.	Spices
	Salt
	Pepper
	Whole Pepper
	Cinnamon
	Cocoa
	Baking Soda
	Bacon Bits
	Baking Powder
	Seasoning Salt
	Mayonnaise
	Mustard
	Ketchup
	Noodles
	Rice
	Wild Rice
	Boxed Potatoes
	Mixes

Qty.	Meat
	Ground Beef
	Steak
	Roast
	Chicken Breast
	Thighs
	Ham
	Lunch Meat
	Pork Chops
	Pork Loin
	Fish
	Shrimp

Qty.	Canned Goods
	Peaches
	Fruit Cocktail
	Chili
	Canned Chicken
	Green Beans
	Peas
	Potatoes
	Carrots
	Corn
	Soups
	Ranch Style Beans
	Baked Beans

Qty.	Fresh Produce
	Lettuce
	Tomatoes
	Potatoes
	Broccoli
	Cucumbers
	Jalepenos
	Onions
	Green Onions
	Bell Peppers
	Bananas
	Oranges
	Apples
	Avocado
	Lemons

Qty.	Others
	Hot Sauce
	Taco Seasoning
	Gum
	Candy

Qty.	Medicine
	B-6
	Allergy PM
	Sinus Allergy AM
	Vitamins
	Nasal Spray

Qty.	Paper Goods
	Foil
	Saran Wrap
	Baggies
	Freezer Bags
	Napkins
	Paper Towels
	Toilet Paper
	Paper Plates
	Waxed Paper
	Toothpicks
	Trash Bags

Qty.	Household
	Bleach
	Tide
	Downy
	Dryer Sheets
	Dawn
	Lever 2000
	Electrasol
	Pledge
	Orange Glo - Floors
	Light Bulbs
	Big Dog Food
	Small Dog Food
	Vacuum Bags
	Windex

Qty.	Personal Items
	Blue Face Pads
	Deodorant
	Small Pads
	Large Pads
	Shampoo
	Conditioner
	Make-up
	Face Powder
	Baby Powder
	Toothpaste
	Toothbrush
	Mouthwash
	Razors

Qty.	Dairy Products
	Spray Whip Cream
	Cream
	Milk
	Yogart
	Eggs
	Cottage Cheese
	Butter
	Tub Butter
	Sour Cream
	Mr. Sharp
	Grated Cheese
	Cream Cheese
	Pudding
	Cheese Whiz

Qty.	Frozen Foods
	Ice Cream
	Pizza
	Whipped Cream
	Pie Crust
	Vegetables
	TV Dinners
	Fish Sticks

Qty.	Breads
	Frozen Rolls
	Loaf Bread
	Hamburger Buns
	Hot Dog Buns
	Chips

Produce

- [ ] Avocados
- [ ] Salad
- [ ] Tomatoes
- [ ] Lemons
- [ ] Oranges
- [ ] Apples
- [ ] Bananas
- [ ] Bell Peppers
- [ ] Potatoes
- [ ] Squash
- [ ] Broccoli
- [ ] Cucumbers
- [ ] Jalepenos
- [ ] Onions
- [ ] Green Onions

Breads

- [ ] Bread
- [ ] HD Buns
- [ ] Ham. Buns
- [ ] Tortillas

Frozen Food 1

- [ ] Pizza
- [ ] Cool Whip
- [ ] Ice Cream
- [ ] Frozen Pies
- [ ] Breakfast
- [ ] Pie Crusts

Frozen Food 2

- [ ] Rolls
- [ ] Green Beans
- [ ] Corn
- [ ] Mixed Veg.
- [ ] Onions…
- [ ] Raviolis
- [ ] Chicken Strips
- [ ] Fish
- [ ] Meatballs
- [ ] Tator Tots
- [ ] French Fries
- [ ] Stir Fry
- [ ] Lasagna
- [ ] Pot Pies
- [ ] Nail Polish

Aisle 3

- [ ] Tea
- [ ] Hot Choc.
- [ ] Coffee
- [ ] Creamer
- [ ] Mayo
- [ ] Ketchup
- [ ] Mustard
- [ ] Choc. Syrup
- [ ] Jelly
- [ ] Peanut butter

Aisle 4

- [ ] Stuffing
- [ ] Boxed Potatoes
- [ ] Hot Sauce
- [ ] Can Corn
- [ ] Can G. Beans
- [ ] Peas
- [ ] Potatoes
- [ ] Spinach
- [ ] Pickles
- [ ] Taco Shells
- [ ] Chalupas
- [ ] Taco Seasoning

Aisle 5

- [ ] Ragu
- [ ] Spaghetti
- [ ] Can Chicken
- [ ] Tuna
- [ ] Parmesan
- [ ] Mac & Cheese
- [ ] Chili
- [ ] Beans
- [ ] Rices
- [ ] Can Tomatoes
- [ ] Rotel
- [ ] Tomato Sauce
- [ ] Hamburger Helper

Aisle 6

- [ ] Can Raviolis
- [ ] Ramen
- [ ] Kool-Aid
- [ ] Soup
- [ ] Broth
- [ ] Can Peaches
- [ ] Can Pineapples

Aisle 7

- [ ] Juice
- [ ] Cookies
- [ ] Crackers
- [ ] PB Crackers
- [ ] PB Cookies
- [ ] Gatorade

Aisle 8

- [ ] Seasonal

Aisle 9

- [ ] Flour
- [ ] Sugar
- [ ] Cake Mix
- [ ] Spices
- [ ] Eagle Brand
- [ ] Coconut
- [ ] Choc. Chips
- [ ] Nuts
- [ ] Oil
- [ ] Jell-O
- [ ] Pudding
- [ ] Bread Mix
- [ ] Yeast
- [ ] Cornbread Mix
- [ ] Graham Crusts

Aisle 10

- [ ] Cereal
- [ ] Breakfast Bars
- [ ] Syrup
- [ ] Oatmeal
- [ ] Grits

Aisle 11

- [ ] Toilet Paper

Aisle 12

- [ ] Napkins
- [ ] Paper Plates
- [ ] Paper Towels
- [ ] Foil
- [ ] Saran
- [ ] Baggies
- [ ] Trash Bags
- [ ] Freezer Bags
- [ ] Toothpicks

Aisle 13

- [ ] Chips
- [ ] Nuts
- [ ] Water
- [ ] Chex Mix
- [ ] Beef Jerky
- [ ] Popcorn

Aisle 14

- [ ] Diet Coke
- [ ] Dr. Pepper

Aisle 15

- [ ] Juice
- [ ] Butter
- [ ] Stick Butter
- [ ] Spray W. Cream
- [ ] Cookie Dough
- [ ] Sour Cream
- [ ] Yogart

Back Wall/Side

- [ ] Milk
- [ ] Cream
- [ ] Eggs

Deli

- [ ] Lunchmeat
- [ ] Cheese
- [ ] Hawaiian Rolls
- [ ] Chicken Strips

Inside Cold

- [ ] Ham
- [ ] Chimichangas
- [ ] Chicken Breasts
- [ ] Chicken Thighs

Far Cold Wall

- [ ] Cream Cheese
- [ ] Grated Cheese
- [ ] Hot Links
- [ ] Hot Dogs
- [ ] Sausage
- [ ] Bacon
- [ ] Chicken
- [ ] Ground Beef
- [ ] Pork Loins
- [ ] Pork Chops

3rd
- [ ] Cologne
- [ ] Bath Gels

4th
- [ ] Shampoo
- [ ] Conditioner
- Hair Gel

5th
- [ ] Brushes
- [ ] Scrunchies

6th
- [ ] Razors
- [ ] Soap
- [ ] Small Pads
- [ ] Maxi Pads
- [ ] Tampons
- [ ] Q-Tips

7th
- [ ] Deodorant
- [ ] Mouthwash
- [ ] Toothpaste
- [ ] Toothbrushes

8th
- [ ] Sinus Allergy PM
- [ ] Cough Drops
- [ ] Lotion
- [ ] Baby Powder
- [ ] Nasal Spray
- [ ] Allergy Med.

9th
- [ ] Vitamin B-6
- [ ] Multivitamin
- [ ] Vitamin C
- [ ] Band-Aids

10th

11th
- [ ] Antacids
- [ ] Gas-X

12th
- [ ] Contact Solution

13th
- [ ] Advil
- [ ] Tylenol

14th
- [ ] Bird Seed
- [ ] Gravel

1st
- [ ] Gum
- [ ] Reeses
- [ ] Candy

2nd
- [ ] Cards

3rd-5th
- [ ] Office Supplies

6th
- [ ] Big Dog Food
- [ ] Little Dog Food

7th
- [ ] Bird Seed
- [ ] Floor Cleaner
- [ ] Pine-Sol
- [ ] Comet
- [ ] Windex
- [ ] Lysol
- [ ] Swiffer Sheets
- [ ] Pledge

8th
- [ ] Dawn
- [ ] Electasol
- [ ] Downy
- [ ] Dryer Sheets
- [ ] Bleach
- [ ] Tide

9th
- [ ] Canning Jars
- [ ] Sure-Jel

10th
- [ ] Trash bags

11th - 12th

13th
- [ ] Small Appliances

14th
- [ ] Appliances
- [ ] Vacuum Bags

15th
- [ ] Lamps
- [ ] Candles

16th
- [ ] Lamp Shades

17th
- [ ] Mirrors

Others
- [ ] Light bulbs
- [ ] Spray Paint
- [ ] Automotive
- [ ] Crafts
- [ ] Shoes
- [ ] Sporting Goods
- [ ] Housing
- [ ] Curtains
- [ ] Women's Clothes
- [ ] Men's Clothes
- [ ] Books
- [ ] Magazines

Household Cleaning Jobs

Dust
Den
Study
Dining
Kitchen
Master
Shea's
Jacob's
Hall Bath
Master Bath

Beds Made
Master
Shea's
Jacob's

Vacuum Carpet

Wood Floors
Vacuum
Mop

Tile Floors (Vacuum & Mop)
Laundry Room
Hall Bath
Master Bath
Kids' Bath

Kitchen
Dishwasher Unloaded
Dishes Washed
Countertops Cleaned
Sink
Table Cleaned

Windowsills

Mirrors
Hall Bath
Master Bath
Kids' Bath
Master Bedroom
Shea's Room
Kitchen
Laundry Room

Laundry
Separated
Washed
Dried
Folded
Put Away
Hung Up

Bathrooms
**Master
Shower
Tub
Sinks
Toilet
**Hall
Sink
Toilet
**Kids'
Sink
Toilet
Tub

Laundry Room
Sink
Top of Washer & Dryer

Baseboards

Birthday Chart

Jan.		May		Sept.	
3	Judy	4	Jay's Christian	12	Meaghan
11	Lance			14	Chris
8	Barbara				
25	Granddaddy				
25	Momma & Daddy				
30	Kristi				
Feb.		**June**		**Oct.**	
12	Lindsey			7	Mine
				16	Tyler
Mar.		**July**			
10	Jacob	1	Jacob's Christian	**Nov.**	
10	W.B. & Linda's	1	Jarrod	1	Harry
15	Greg	28	Adrian's Christian	7	Adrian
16	Our Anniversary	28	Madison	11	Shea
22	W.B.			29	Momma
27	Granny				
Apr.		**Aug.**		**Dec.**	
10	Kristie	3	Rebecca	4	Linda
10	Neenie	7	Daddy		
14	My Christian	12	Grant		
20	Jay	28	Molly		
25	Sherri				

		Birthday Chart		
Jan.		May	Sept.	
Feb.		June	Oct.	
Mar.		July	Nov.	
Apr.		Aug.	Dec.	

Resources

I applied my heart to what I observed,
And learned a lesson from what I saw.
Proverbs 24:32

That everyone may eat and drink, and find satisfaction in
All his toil – this is the gift of God.
Ecclesiastes 3:13

Books

Barnes, Emilie. The Creative Home Organizer. Oregon: Harvest House
 Publishers, 1988.

Barnes, Emilie. More Hours in My Day. Oregon: Harvest House Publishers,
 2002.

Burnside, Diane, ed. Pillsbury Kitchens' Cookbook. Minneapolis,
 Minnesota: The Pillsbury Company, 1984.

Hallam, Linda, ed. Better Homes and Gardens: Making a Home.
 Des Moines: Meredith Corporation, 2001.

Kerr Home Canning and Freezing Book. Kerr Glass Manufacturing Corp.
 Sand Springs, Oklahoma.

Lees, Christopher MD, Reynolds, Karina MD, & McCartan, Grainne.
 Pregnancy and Birth, Your Questions Answered. Canada: Friefly
 Books, 2002.

Martin, Kimberly. Cooking for College Dummies. Self-Published, 2004.

Reader's Digest. Household Hints & Handy Tips. Pleasantville,
 New York: Reader's Digest Association, 1988.

Wilson, P.B. God is in the Kitchen Too. Oregon: Harvest House
 Publishers, 2003.

Websites

www.cookingvillage.com

www.kraftfoods.com

www.busycooks.com

Local Consultants/Organizations as Resources

These are a few home parties/business that are found locally. Many ideas in each area are given during the parties. The parties are held in your home, and usually last about 2 hours. By hosting a party, you get to socialize with friends and family, take in ideas, and receive free merchandise.

Also, if you are looking to make a little extra money in your own time, these home parties may be what you are looking for.

Home Interior

Avon

Mary Kay

Homemade Gourmet

Pampered Chef

Candle Lites

Sandy Clough Tea Parties

For more information about Susan Sikes' seminars or speaking engagements, please contact:

Out of the Nest & Beyond
3196 Ridgeview Rd.
Caddo Mills, TX 75135
903-527-4148
903-450-6996
www.outofthenestandbeyond.com

CPSIA information can be obtained
at www.ICGtesting.com
Printed in the USA
LVHW062352100523
746704LV00012B/636